FINE
BOOKBINDING
In the Twentieth Century

FINE BOOKBINDING
In the Twentieth Century

Roy Harley Lewis

With 33 color and 82 monochrome illustrations

ARCO PUBLISHING, INC.
New York

Published 1985 by Arco Publishing, Inc.
215 Park Avenue South, New York, NY 10003

Text © Roy Harley Lewis 1984

Library of Congress Cataloging in Publication Data

Lewis, Roy Harley.
    Fine bookbinding in the twentieth century.

    Bibliography: p.
    Includes index.
    1. Bookbinding – History – 20th century.   2. Bookbinding
– Ornamental bindings.   I. Title.   II. Title: Fine
bookbinding in the 20th century.
Z269.L5   1984   686.3′09′04   84–9375
ISBN 0-668-06084-0

Printed in Great Britain

CONTENTS

INTRODUCTION

An old proverb maintains that nothing is new except what has been forgotten, and this is especially appropriate in the arts, where little is truly original. Yet from time to time there emerges a craftsman who continues to strive for a degree of originality, and through inspiration or experimentation succeeds in creating a style or movement that is different enough to extend the existing frontiers. The latter half of this century has seen a renaissance in bookbinding, and today there is a growing number of men and women reaching for new dimensions, and by so doing raising standards to new peaks. Only time can put this work in proper perspective, so lasting judgements will have to be deferred until the next century. Meanwhile, some of the bookbinding we are seeing today is more exciting than anything to date in the lifetimes of most of us.

Some of the 'modern' work that has appeared in recent years has been motivated – not always knowingly - by what has gone before. The influences of the past are inevitable; yet ideas freshly handled can still be novel and interesting. This book is about craftsmanship as well as artistry and innovation, and who is to say that even a blatant copy does not have some merit if judged on that basis? Earlier in the century there was a fashion for sumptuously decorated, jewelled bindings. It could be said that this was merely a sophisticated imitation of the Byzantine style, but that would be unfair to the twentieth-century craftsmen. The product of different worlds, there was little common ground on which the bindings might be compared.

There was a time when leather bindings were so commonplace that books could be purchased by the yard as furnishings, along with curtains and carpets. With the gradual disappearance of the old-style craftsmen, and the soaring cost of leather, considerably more respect has been shown to the leather-bound book. But with *fine* bindings, sought and collected for their beauty or (in artistic terms) significance, the changes have been more far-reaching. Not only did it become increasingly difficult to try to match the masterpieces of earlier centuries, but collectors began to look for something less stereotyped than the familiar range of traditional bindings. Their education in what was now possible was left to a handful of creative binders who refused to accept the constraints of tradition.

There are two schools of fine hand binding: the traditional 'trade' craftsmen who produce about 90 per cent of the industry's total output, and the creative individual, or small unit, who produce one-off bindings for collectors and museums, often through exhibitions. There have always been brilliant individual craftsmen (and this included many who worked in anonymity for the larger firms), but it was not until the 1960s that there was a recognisable movement towards innovative binding.

Since the 1950s, no doubt benefitting from the shot-in-the-arm provided by the Festival of Britain to so many arts and crafts (in Britain), interest in 'modern' bookbinding has been gathering momentum, and remarkable work is coming from England, from France where the seeds first took root, from the United States, where tremendous artistic energy is being expended, and from much of Europe, including the Communist bloc, particularly Czechoslovakia.

Though only a relatively limited number of collectors can afford to commission a binding at between £500 and £5,000 there is considerable investment potential in something which is obviously unique and, as with the book itself, there are always a few ready to pay large amounts for something special. Shakespeare's *King Lear*, bound by one of the most brilliant designer-bookbinders, Philip Smith, was sold on completion in 1967 for £566. Ten years later it was resold for £6,000, and today, bearing in mind that experts, including some of Smith's competitors, regard it as the outstanding binding of the past three decades, the price would be substantially more.

Bookbinding as a craft has evolved to such an extent that a re-examination of many familiar trade terms is

A binding not constrained by tradition. For the tall, narrow *Fungus and Curmudgeonly*, by Simon Meyerson, Sally Lou Smith incorporated in her 1982 binding a cassette recording of the two-character play in a linen sack on the front cover. The binding, in black and turquoise goatskin, is influenced by the illustrations of Natalia d'Arbeloff, which are deep-etched with various woven textures in turquoise, black and grey. Note the mesh blocking on the back cover.

8

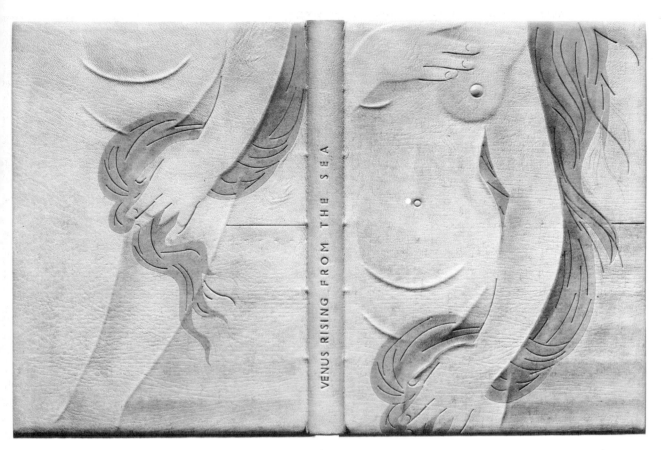

Venus Rising from the Sea, by Arnold Bennett. Trevor Jones's remarkable design (1973) can be studied on two levels: first as a projection of the title, and second as an interplay of real and illusory three-dimensionality, shapes being built up on the leather with dye, and under the leather with layers of card and lino parings. As the book is turned in the hand, real and painted shadows sometimes work in unison, sometimes contradict each other. Jones usually designs different fronts and backs; often his designs are asymmetric, continuing across both boards and spine. Since Venus is rising from the sea, she is higher on the back of the book. The title also 'rises' on the spine.

overdue, and none more than 'fine' binding, which has to cover such varying creations. Definitions need to be more precise when movements become fragmented. The interests and philosophies of modern binders differ widely. One might be comparing bindings whose only common feature is that they are the work of professionals applying the same basic skills. Donald Glaister, one of the younger American school, puts the issue in perspective in a down-to-earth observation on what constitutes 'fine' binding.

There could be a book without a design binding, obviously. There could also be a story or idea passed on without printing: handwriting will do the job. Photocopying a manuscript or typescript transmits the written word, and even transmits illustrations, quite well. We don't need hand-made paper or anything so expensive or fancy as that; what comes out of the copy machine is all right. As to binding, staples and coloured paper will work. There is nothing wrong with a book that is produced by xeroxing and stapling. It is just not a finely made book. In my opinion, a fine book without a fine binding is not complete; it is not an integrated whole. It is only 'fine' as far as it goes. My job is to take it to completion.

However, in the general context, 'fine binding' is still the most appropriate description when taken to mean what is best – in whatever style, or in whatever movement.

One of the problems encountered in compiling this study has been in defining the term 'binder', because the traditional or dictionary definition of 'fastening sheets of a book into a cover, especially of leather' is only part of the story. Of course, many hand binders are concerned only with repairing old books, but in our context the criterion is the ability to produce one-off or limited-edition works in which the cover 'decoration' is usually the most influential factor. This is not splitting hairs, because some of the most famous names in binding have been designers whose working knowledge of the craft was little more than superficial. How does one compare a brilliant and influential artist like Paul Bonet, whose work inspired not only his contemporaries but those who followed, with others

9

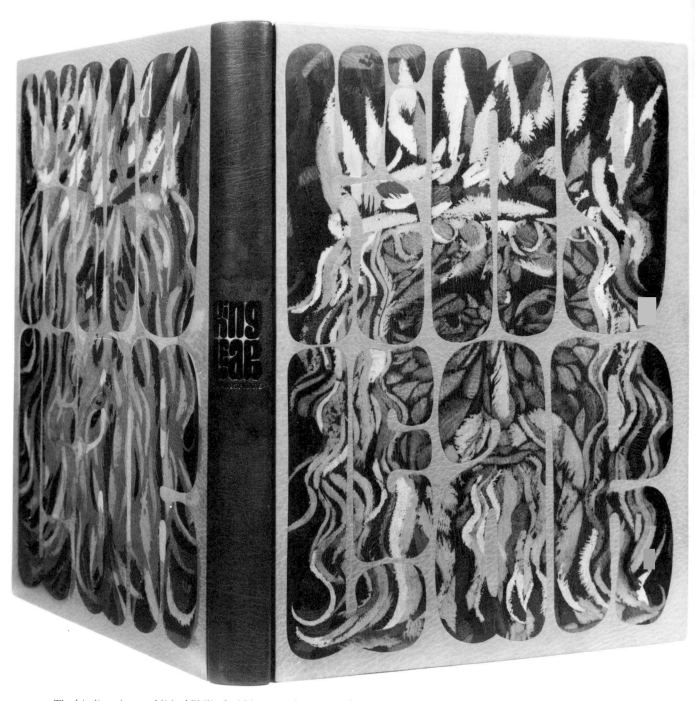

The binding that established Philip Smith's reputation as an artist
of special talent: *King Lear*. Notice that the lower board shows the
back of Lear's head.

who have made major contributions in both structure and decoration? Opinions differ. Significantly, binders with an arts (as opposed to crafts) background tend to dismiss the division as unimportant, despite the fact that this in some way contradicts the spirit of modern binding – as expounded by men like Cobden-Sanderson – in which one person sees the whole process through from start to finish.

My intention is to illustrate some of the best work of the century, ranging from conventional to avant-garde. Some of those included produce work that is mainstream: though it is highly attractive and displays immaculate craftsmanship, their contribution to binding lies partly in their role as teachers. The interaction between teacher and pupil is not only fascinating, but often surprising.

Even what is loosely termed 'the modern movement' is not as cohesive as it might seem on the surface. One of the guiding principles is that a book's cover should be (in simple terms) an extension of the author's message, and this is accepted by almost all hand binders, whatever their views on the speed at which some changes in emphasis are being made. Yet a notable exception is Ivor Robinson, a man at the very forefront of the movement and a past President of the

distinguished body of Designer Bookbinders. He believes the very opposite – that a binding should stand on its own; that the author is frequently just one contributor to the total book (no more important than the person who made the paper, selected and set the print, or did the illustrations), and that it can even be pretentious to endeavour to interpret works of great complexity (such as those of Dante). This interesting argument is developed in Chapter 4.

This book pays tribute to some of the outstanding firms and individuals, illustrating highlights of the work that has emerged, as well as indicating trends and developments. The newest fashion in the United States, for example, is what has become known as the 'total' book: the craftsperson might produce not only the binding, but the paper, typefaces, illustrations and even text (a concept not far removed from principles followed by William Morris a hundred years ago). But since the quality of interesting works of creation does not always match the consuming integrity and enthusiasm for the philosophy, I have touched on it only in passing. Many of the binders featured continue

Edgar Mansfield's binding for *In the Heart of the Country*, showing use of inlay as well as tooling.

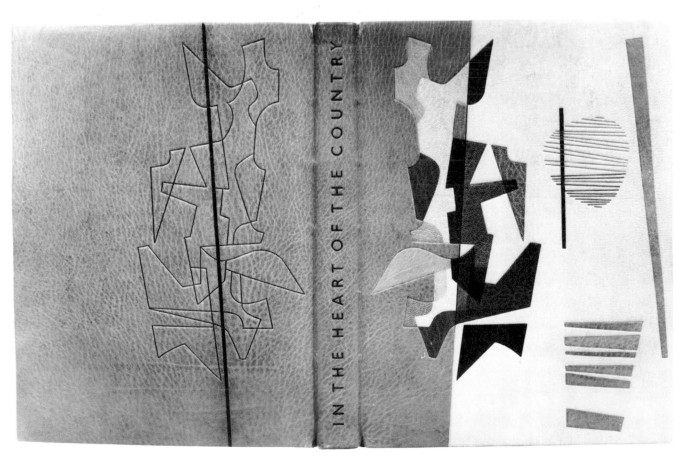

to experiment, but never at the expense of their standards of craftsmanship, or jeopardising the function of the book.

Modern binding is an art form, but its status among the other arts — particularly painting — is still debatable. Even the more art-orientated binders are divided on this issue, and on how they see themselves; with the craft as a whole, the difference in attitudes — artistic and philosophical — is naturally much greater. For instance Edgar Mansfield, considered by many to be the 'father' of the modern movement, is dismissed by one critic — a distinguished binder — as 'merely a decorator'. So to make major critical judgements you have to select a stance among all this, which is not the task of this book. My selection of individuals representing the modern movement is to some extent personal, occasionally limited by difficulties in communication with individuals, especially in Eastern Europe. The men and women included have produced work of a standard acknowledged as outstanding by their peers, and they make a significant contribution to the development of the art — or, as some would prefer, the craft.

I must thank Bernard Middleton who checked the manuscript for errors and misconceptions, Philip Smith for encouragement and general advice, Dr Mirjam Foot of the British Library, Jane Rick of the Victoria and Albert Museum, Richard Sawyer (Charles J. Sawyer), and Bryan Maggs (Maggs Bros) for help with photographic research, and Mary Lamb of Harmatan Leather for translating Dutch and Flemish material. Thanks are also due to the many photographers whose work is shown, including Michael Barrett, Tony Evans, Fell-Hurworth Photography, Sidney Pizan.

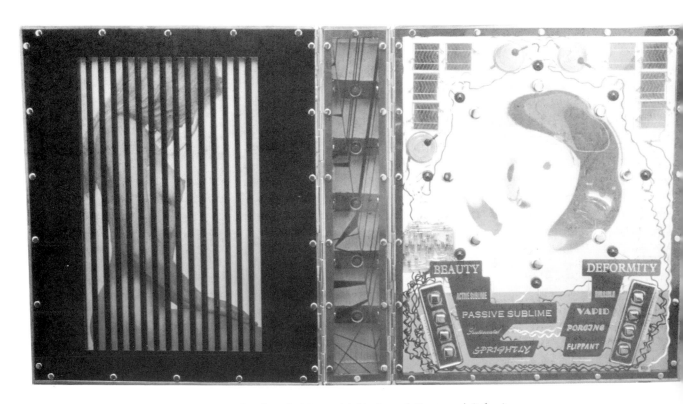

James Brockman's 'electronic' binding of *Beauty and Deformity* (see page 48).

1

THE BACKGROUND

The craft of bookbinding started, as so many things did, with the monks, the only group in society who had the leisure time and, more important, the education. As early as the sixth century, English monks were protecting manuscripts by placing them between boards sewn together. Their novel idea of decorating the boards with metal and jewels was relatively short-lived: for every person who could read there were hundreds who preferred more profitable pastimes – so the most attractive features of many bound manuscripts were the jewels set in the cover, easily prised from their wooden settings. To make matters worse, having suspicious minds, 'collectors' would assume that other precious stones had been concealed, and they were not satisfied until the covers had been whittled down to a pile of wood shavings – simple avarice rather than vandalism, which is a relatively recent characteristic of the so-called civilised races.

As history has shown, the monks were shrewd, amassing great wealth in art treasures. Between the tenth and fourteenth centuries, having copied and developed the designs of 'books' brought from the East, they became Europe's foremost binders. By now they were moulding leather over the boards, and decorating with the impressions of metal stamps, or seals.

The first breakthrough came with the introduction of the printing press in the fifteenth century. Because of the bottleneck of material being transcribed by machine (the enormous wealth of manuscript material dating back to ancient Greece and Rome on which the early printers embarked is mind-boggling), the roles of printer and binder began to diverge. Within a short period the binder came into his own, and with the aid of new delicate tools for impressing designs on the leather, a new skill was born. The history of binding from that time is basically the history of book-cover design; binding techniques were to change little.

It was in Venice in the sixteenth century that the art developed (along with printing), although Jean Grolier (1479–1565) took the skill back to France, to establish a proud tradition which has kept that country in the forefront of hand binding ever since. For the next 200 years France set the pace, followed by Germany. In England it was Royal patronage which contributed to the growth of the craft, and among the men whose work survives to this day were Thomas Berthelet, binder to Henry VIII, John Gibson who worked in the reign of James I, and Samuel Mearne, binder to Charles II. He was the first binder in Britain to make gold tooling fashionable, although it had been used widely since 1520. As the king's bookseller and stationer he was in a good position to influence others. His 'cottage' style, with its angled geometric patterns at the top and bottom of the book's panels, was used from 1660 and widely copied, not always with the same degree of craftsmanship.

Towards the end of the next century, Roger Payne (1738–97) took cover decoration a step forward by designing his own range of tools (for *impressing* decorative marks, as opposed to *cutting*), and limiting that tooling in the main to delicate cornerpieces and borders, always endeavouring to maintain what he considered to be the 'character' of the book. It is a tribute to Payne that his work began to be copied by French binders, who had dominated the binding scene for so long. It was also a period of ingenuity, not to say gimmickry. James Edwards, of one of the more important trade binderies, Edwards of Halifax, patented (in 1785) a method of binding in vellum decorated with painted scenes. Edwards' breakthrough was in their ability to capitalise on the transparency of specially prepared vellum, so that by mounting the painting in reverse on the underside, it showed through, and was indestructible. The idea was novel enough to be imitated over a century later when Cedric Chivers of Bath introduced the 'Vellucent' trade name for a method of painting on the paper with which the vellum was lined. Not surprisingly the later version was somewhat debased, for a different kind of market. About the same time, G. T. Bagguley of Newcastle-

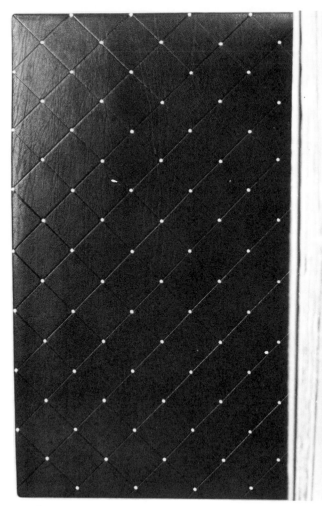

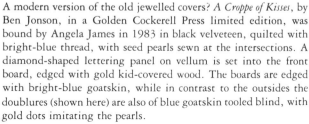

A modern version of the old jewelled covers? *A Croppe of Kisses*, by Ben Jonson, in a Golden Cockerell Press limited edition, was bound by Angela James in 1983 in black velveteen, quilted with bright-blue thread, with seed pearls sewn at the intersections. A diamond-shaped lettering panel on vellum is set into the front board, edged with gold kid-covered wood. The boards are edged with bright-blue goatskin, while in contrast to the outsides the doublures (shown here) are also of blue goatskin tooled blind, with gold dots imitating the pearls.

under-Lyme, another distinguished company, produced what was known as the 'Sutherland tooling process' (named after one of the their customers, the Duchess of Sutherland). This was a novel method of tooling colour as a design feature on the surface of vellum, for use mainly as doublures, the inside faces of the covers.

However, these were merely ripples which had little real effect on the mainstream of fine binding. By the 1840s the trade was forced to put its house in order by the earlier appearance of an insidious rival to leather: cloth, coupled with the arrival of a major new technique in trade binding. The result was similar to

the effect of TV on the film industry a century later; the traditional industry in the process of contracting was obliged to improve the quality of its work. A publisher, William Pickering, had introduced cloth twenty years before, and it was soon realised that covers and printed sheets could be prepared separately by machine and *glued* (instead of sewn) together. It was the clothbound book which met the boom in demand created by advances in education in that period.

Craft binders working at the lower end of the market could no longer compete, but the better firms were to enjoy a period of affluence, and with them a new breed of private binder who brought a freshness of approach – which set the cat among the pigeons, but which made hand binding what it has become today. Outstanding among them was T. J. Cobden-Sanderson (1841–1922) destined to become one of the great names in modern craft binding. It is with him, against the lush backcloth provided by his traditional but technically brilliant contemporaries, that the story begins.

14

2
THE EARLY DAYS OF THE CENTURY

The development of any art form is never even; it moves in fits and starts in direct relation to the talent of those engaged in it at any one period. But individuals with such a wealth of talent, or the ability to inspire others through their teaching, appear as infrequently as new stars in the galaxy. In the eighty-odd years of this century there have been only three or four in the binding field, although it is to be hoped that some of the younger craftsmen beginning to emerge will develop into very special binders. It is perhaps Philip Smith, a former President of Designer Bookbinders, who – demonstrating by example and motivated by a sometimes controversial but always fascinating philosophy – is the latest to blaze a trail bright enough for others to follow. He in turn was motivated by Edgar Mansfield, who had an even greater impact in the 1950s when he stood alone. Before him the standards were set by Douglas Cockerell. But it all began with T. J. Cobden-Sanderson.

The ambiguity of the word 'original' has already been raised. Although many of the craftsmen featured in this history are (or were) forward thinkers, in many ways Cobden-Sanderson was a traditionalist – yet his ideas were resisted, even ridiculed by most of his contemporaries. What was it that made him so different?

His name always evokes that of William Morris (1834–96), the English poet and painter, because of their work together at the Kelmscott Press in the 1890s; yet for all their common love of beauty their styles were very different. The reputation of Morris, one of the leaders of the Pre-Raphaelite Brotherhood, was already established when he founded his now famous private press. The Kelmscott edition of Chaucer epitomises the peaks of artistic achievement sought and usually accomplished by Morris. To give its publication date, 1896, dismisses the incredible effort and talent poured into the book – which took nearly five years to prepare, three and a half years to execute, and twenty-one months to print. Limited to 425

It is not easy to see books bound by T. J. Cobden-Sanderson because he stopped binding in 1893, although he continued to design for the Doves Bindery for many more years. *Poems, Selected from Percy Bysshe Shelley* was one of the last – a birthday present that year for his daughter Stella, hence the initial S which is a feature. The tooling, on a navy-blue background, is in gold, and there is a blind-tooled floral pattern on the gilt edges. *(Bodleian Library)*

15

copies, with 46 supervised by Cobden-Sanderson at the Doves Bindery, it is hardly surprising that good copies today could fetch £10,000 – say $15,000. Consider the following: 87 illustrations by Edward Burne-Jones; 1 full-page woodcut title (the book size was 15 × 10¾in); 14 large borders; 18 frames for pictures; 26 large initial words, all designed by Morris, plus smaller initials; and designs for binding in white pigskin, with silver clasps, executed by Douglas Cockerell (then apprenticed to the bindery).

Cobden-Sanderson brought a fresh approach to book production, possibly because he came to it relatively late in life with a mind uncluttered with precedent and awareness of technical limitations. At seventeen he was apprenticed as an engineer, but he decided he did not like business and read for Cambridge with the intention of entering the church. But, at Trinity College, he studied mathematics for three years, opting out at the last moment before taking his degree because he objected to the competitive exam system. Of independent means he was able to devote himself for the next seven or eight years to the study of Carlyle and of literature, concentrating on German philosophy. At the beginning of the 1880s he was finishing an exhausting stint revising the bylaws of a railway, and looked round desperately for a complete contrast. It was William Morris's wife who encouraged him to take up bookbinding.

Having taken a six-month 'apprenticeship' with Roger de Coverly, he set up on his own, until establishing the Doves Bindery in 1893. Traditionally, bookbinding had been split into specialist functions, men being trained either to work as *forwarders* (binding the book) or as *finishers* (decorating the covers), and as a newcomer Cobden-Sanderson upset the trade by choosing to do everything himself. Today there is still a difference of opinion between traditionalists who believe that no one person working alone can match the narrow specialist expertise of the best craftsmen from one of the few remaining large trade binderies, and individual hand binders who maintain that if there is any minute difference in quality it is more than offset by the advantages of continuity. The debate may never be resolved, but its importance is far less than might be imagined. Certainly some of Cobden-Sanderson's early work, due to his inexperience, was not up to the highest technical standards. But, by applying himself to basics with all the fervour of a man with a mission, he brought a refreshing integrity to the craft in the structural as well as artistic sense.

Cobden-Sanderson was a visionary, respected more for his ideals and principles than his own craftsmanship, and he seemed to lose a degree of interest in the actual physical binding work once he had established a commercial enterprise in which he could leave it to the talented assistants he had gathered around him. He had, however, discovered an aptitude for gold tooling and this was used to effect in very simple 'clean' designs at a time when it seemed that every available inch of leather had to be decorated in one manner or another.

The reputation of the Doves Bindery was built and sustained by his conviction that the work they were doing was something far more important than attaching covers to a book, by his decisions about 'clean' designs, and by his insistence on a return to the highest standards of craftsmanship – which meant refusing to cheat by the use of inferior leathers, or the attachment of false raised bands to hollow backs made with waste paper of low quality, or overcasting too-thick paper.

It has been said, even by his admirers, that Cobden-Sanderson's designs were derivative, and if one searches for long enough one can find similar patterns from earlier centuries, eg the delicate tooling of Roger Payne, or a seventeenth-century French binder, Le Gascon. But he was too much his own man to copy anyone. He was, after all, a disciple of William Morris, yet when he formed the Doves Press in 1900 the style of the books as a whole could not be more different – simple to the point of austerity, compared with the romantic ornateness of the Kelmscott Press. 'I always give greater attention in the typography of a book, to what I leave out than what I put in,' he said.

Indeed, the principal Doves type has been hailed as one of the most graceful typefaces in existence – or to be accurate, once in existence, because Cobden-Sanderson threw the original pieces of the beautiful Emery Walker typeface which he used for his great printing masterpiece, *The Doves Bible* (1905), in the River Thames. It is not clear whether this was the aftermath of a bitter quarrel with Walker, or some symbolic gesture more related to the burial of Excalibur in the Arthurian legend than to the twentieth century. Perhaps the latter is more in keeping with this man, who practised yoga when it was little known in the West, and had many mystical interests; a man considered so absent-minded that, while he might remember to keep an appointment, it was seldom on the right day! An eccentric, but not the sort of man who could allow himself knowingly to copy another's designs.

A fairly typical Doves binding, *Pericles and Aspasia*, by W. S. Landor, was designed by Cobden-Sanderson and bound at the Doves Bindery in 1904. Blue morocco and gold tooling. (*Victoria & Albert Museum*)

Because of his dreams of perfection, Cobden-Sanderson was very conscious of the content of a book – reverent of a fine text, dismissive of what he considered of no value. In fact, he complained about the 'poor' books his customers brought to be bound. He had little idea that with the high cost of one-off bindings similar questions would be raised in the 1980s, ie how often can collectors afford to pay anything up to £5,000 for a binding, no matter how impressive, if the book itself is of little consequence?

Cobden-Sanderson inspired a movement in which talented individuals were able to offer an alternative to the traditional designs from the trade binderies. From guilds, formed as semi-amateurs gained in confidence and expertise, there eventually emerged the highly respected society of Designer Bookbinders of today, ensuring through constant monitoring that individuals as well as the trade cannot again become complacent.

Cobden-Sanderson's designs – 2,000 separate patterns and records of 816 books bound between 1884 and 1905 – in the form of rubbings taken by Charles McLeish (Snr), are now in the Bodleian Library, Oxford, as part of the famous Broxbourne Library collection of Albert Ehrman. The rubbings were subsequently bound in five huge volumes for Ehrman by Charles McLeish (Jnr). (The Broxbourne collection of fine bindings from the twelfth to twentieth centuries was so named because Ehrman, a dedicated and scholarly collector, lived at Broxbourne (Herts) in the 1920s. From 1938 it was housed at his later home, near Beaulieu (Hants), and on his death was given to the Bodleian, the library of Oxford University – second in size in Britain only to the British Library.)

It would be wrong to assume that the old-established trade binderies were not still producing work of the highest craftsmanship. Indeed, some of the trade binders, whether forwarders or finishers, were outstanding craftsmen, though overlooked because they were anonymous cogs in large units. Profiting from a minor boom caused by the fashion of taking paperbound acquisitions to one's personal binder, there were at the start of the century, several large British firms employing up to 100 skilled men. Most customers, admittedly, would be sufficiently impressed with the fashionable cover designs currently available – which could be as varied as the firm's range of decorative tools. To this day, the heavy cost of such hand tools has meant that the few remaining old binderies have cornered the market in the repair of some old volumes, simply because they remain the only people with access to the original equipment. (Some years ago an American collector complained to me about the inferior workmanship on part of a set of books

he had sent to a European firm for rebinding, but when in due course other items in the set needed repair he was obliged to go back to the same bindery, because of the unique tooling pattern, which only they could match.)

But in the binding of limited editions of, for instance, expensive colour-plate books, there was greater scope for creating new designs, albeit in a conventional idiom. Because of the skill of the craftsmen involved – seldom identified in an age when such talent was taken for granted – the results were often dazzling works of art. These sumptuous cover designs generally bore little relation to the content of the book, and were usually the same, whether on a new publication or one hundreds of years old. However, if one discounts the integrity demanded by most modern binders, who insist that a binding should be an extension of the author's intent, many remain examples of superb craftsmanship. Most of this work was carried out by firms like Zaehnsdorf, George Bayntun, Robert Rivière & Son, Fazakerly, Sangorski & Sutcliffe and W. T. Morrell, most of whom have disappeared, the latter as recently as 1983.

The oldest surviving firm in this distinguished group was founded by Hungarian-born Joseph Zaehnsdorf (1814–86), who worked as a binder in Austria, Switzerland, Germany and France before joining his brother, a London jeweller, for a family reunion in 1837. Deciding to stay, he worked for other binders, including the outstanding London firm of the time, Mackenzie, before setting up on his own in 1842. It was an uphill battle to become established but the business prospered and its reputation was made by the time he handed over to his son, Joseph William Zaehnsdorf. Young Joseph was sent to school in France, and apprenticed to a German bindery, before the Franco-Prussian war forced him to return home. His training was completed under the expert eye of his father. He had a flair for promotion, as well as a talent for the craft, and when his book *The Art of Bookbinding* – the definitive work on the subject for many years – was published in 1880, he was still only twenty-eight.

At the turn of the century the company, which had risen to the forefront of Europe's leading binderies, was employing 120 people; the culmination of its prestige was its appointment as bookbinders to Edward VII, as both Prince of Wales and as King. Ernest, grandson of the founder, took over from 1920 until the end of World War II, but the industry as a whole was in decline, and eventually control passed into outside hands; at one time it was owned by Hatchards, the distinguished London booksellers. In 1955 it was taken over by George Rainbird, better known today as the man who introduced 'packaging' to the British publishing industry. Having whet his appetite with the smaller Wigmore Bindery, Rainbird and his friend and colleague Bob Moody set about rejuvenating the firm – aided by a company name still good enough to win prestige orders, such as the provision of all the service books for the new Coventry Cathedral, and the World War II Roll of Honour for the US Merchant Navy, compiled over a ten-year period.

In 1965 Rainbird was joined by his son Tony, returning from a four-year spell in the United States, where his business experience included selling encyclopaedias door to door. Tony had always had an affinity for binding, and had chosen to work in a bindery during his school holidays. Eight years later he took over the reins, enabling his father to concentrate on his publishing interests. Soon after the business was acquired by Colonel Philip Bradfer-Lawrence, former managing director of a leading firm of brewers, a close friend of the family and keen amateur binder and collector, who took over as chairman, but was succeeded by Tony Rainbird in 1983.

Today, the skilled workforce numbers 28, which probably makes Zaehnsdorf the largest employer of skilled binders after the British Library. To meet the high overheads of their factory in Bermondsey, South London, they are happy to take on run-of-the-mill work such as project engineers' 'bibles' (which can be as many as twenty volumes containing the detailed costings on major engineering or building schemes). A stranger order that came in 1983 was to rebind 1,160 books for a private library in Greece, the only instruction being to use leather in the three colours of the library decor – white, ivory and dark grey; this is surely a reversion to using books solely as furnishings.

Zaehnsdorf's main interest is limited editions. Rainbird and his colleagues may decide to produce five or six copies of some particular book and offer them to likely collectors or a publishing firm may commission

The firm of Zaehnsdorf bound five copies of *The Australian Flower Paintings of Ferdinand Bauer* in 1977. Designed and executed by Frederick Glazebrook, finished by Pat Flint.

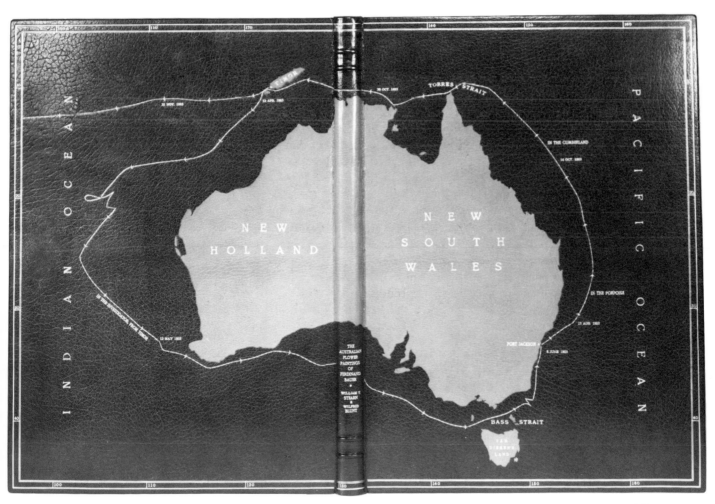

an edition of several hundred copies, often facsimiles of some valuable book, for example they bound a three-volume set (two of text, one matching box of drawings) of Leonardo da Vinci's *Anatomical Studies*, from the Queen's collection at Windsor, a ten-year project of Johnson Reprint (a subsidiary of Harcourt Brace Jovanovich of New York), which will in due course include similar editions of da Vinci's landscapes, horses and portraits. The order, worth £500,000 ($750,000), entailed the full-leather binding of 500 English-language sets; 350 three-quarter leather sets for Japan; and 300 for Germany. Since the size of the books is around $13 \times 19 \times 3\frac{1}{4}$in, the materials alone cost £95,000, around $142,000 (the royal blue Chieftain goatskin, bigger than Nigerian goatskin, was £2.65 or $4 a foot at the time of purchase), and gold leaf £6,000 (about $9,000). The retail price of each set in 1983 was £3,000 (about $4,500).

Two years earlier, Zaehnsdorf handled a smaller but more lavishly produced binding for a limited edition (1,000 sets) of the works of Abdul Aziz Al Saud, the company's first major export order. It was estimated that the assembly of a portfolio containing 58 prints and two volumes, measuring $24\frac{1}{2} \times 18\frac{3}{4} \times 2\frac{1}{4}$in, took craftsmen a total of 14,713 *hand* working hours (equivalent to 7.07 years' work for one person), and that does not include the highly specialist work of gilding the edges (solid gilding in $23\frac{1}{4}$ carat gold leaf), which was sub-contracted to a specialist firm. The bizarre climax to the story is that half the order (500 sets) was sold to a Saudi Arabian prince who subsequently had the whole consignment destroyed – because he did not like the paintings! What he thought of the bindings, which won the printing industry's annual Bain Hogg award, is not known.

In contrast to Zaehnsdorf's early struggle, its greatest rivals, Sangorski & Sutcliffe, were successful so quickly that it is commonly believed they were also founded in the nineteenth century, instead of 1901; another reason is that the reputations of the partners, Frank Sangorski and George Herbert Sutcliffe, had preceded them. Meeting as students at London's Central School of Arts & Crafts, their principal influence was Douglas Cockerell (a protégé of Cobden-Sanderson), for whom they later worked for a year. In 1900 they were appointed teachers at the Camberwell School of Art & Crafts, and the following year started their own business from an attic room in Bloomsbury. Their first commission was a presentation volume from Parliament to Earl Roberts, on the death in battle of his last surviving son. Within a year they were asked to bind the service books for the coronation of King Edward VII. Almost immediately they were given

other prestige commissions, such as the binding of a lectern bible which Edward VII sent to the United States to commemorate the tercentenary of the English church there.

But the partners, fired by the romantic tradition of William Morris (through Douglas Cockerell, who had worked on the Kelmscott *Chaucer*), were restless to leave their mark with something that might be judged a masterpiece. It was the visionary quality of Fitzgerald's *Rubáiyát of Omar Khayyám*, and their admiration for the magnificent jewelled volumes of the Renaissance that inspired them, when approached by John Harrison Stonehouse, a director of Henry Sotheran, the eminent antiquarian booksellers, to undertake what was to be hailed as the 'greatest modern binding in the world'. Any such claim is always extravagant, but what Sangorski & Sutcliffe produced was a remarkable work of art. It is somehow fitting that its story reads like an extract from *Stranger Than Fiction*.

Working on the large Vedder edition of *Omar*, Frank Sangorski's design for the front cover featured a peacock, which was to become a recognisable symbol of the firm's work; the black and white photography of the period does not do it justice. Statistics relating to the constituent parts in a binding are not usually important, compared with the use that is made of them, but in this instance they do illustrate the size of the task undertaken. Five thousand separate pieces of leather were used for the intricate onlay work, 100 square feet of gold leaf, and 1,051 semi-precious stones; and the eye of the snake on the *inside* of the front cover was an emerald. The binding was executed by Sylvester Byrnes, who had joined the firm two years after its start and was regarded as the country's best forwarder, and finished by George Lovett, who made his own tools.

The partners and Sotheran's were delighted with the result; but alarmed at the cost – £1,000, a small fortune in 1912 – Mr Stonehouse decided to put the book up for auction. Whatever his reasons for wanting to sell quickly, he chose the wrong time; there was a major coal strike to add to the economic gloom, and the *Omar* was knocked down for the disappointing figure of £400. (NB the weekly wage of a top craftsman in 1912 was £2, compared with little short of £200 today.)

In April of that year the book started its journey to its new owner in the United States on the world's largest liner, the 'unsinkable' *Titanic*. The destruction of the fabulous binding made headlines – even alongside the loss of 1,600 lives. There is an ancient superstition that peacocks are unlucky, and while we

Sangorski & Sutcliffe did this double binding of Tennyson poems in 1910. Lower picture shows the doublures.

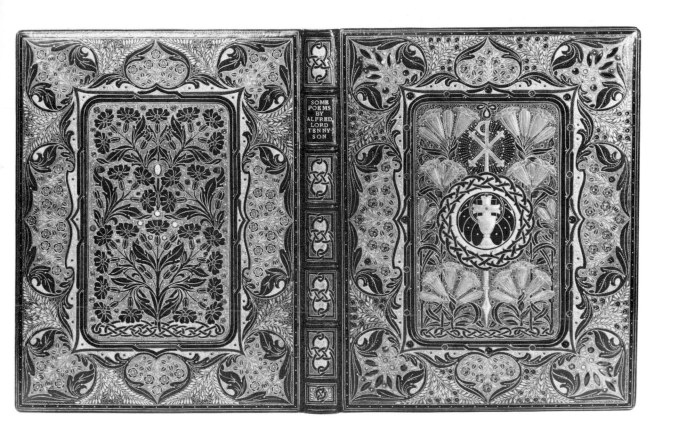

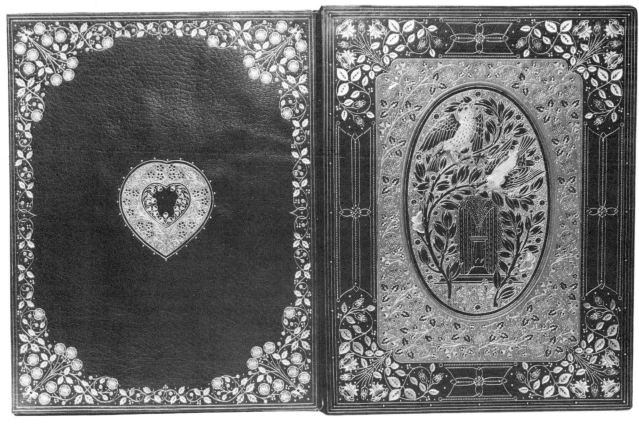

21

22

scoff at such tales, it has to be noted that Frank Sangorski died at the age of thirty-seven only six weeks later, in a bathing accident off the Sussex coast – to be followed within a few months by George Lovett's death from tuberculosis. And who is to say that fate did not play a hand several years later when the company tried to re-create the peacock-decorated *Omar*?

George Sutcliffe continued to run the business, on his own, and in 1924 brought in his seventeen-year-old nephew, Stanley Bray, as an apprentice. Bray showed a natural talent and in due course became a partner, inheriting the firm on Sutcliffe's death in 1943. He is still active today, although the company was taken over in 1978 by Asprey, the London jewellers. Contraction was inevitable as the whole industry suffered from the limited demands of a changing society. At the height of its success in the late 1920s and early 1930s, Sangorski & Sutcliffe employed eighty skilled staff. Today there are only a handful.

Back in 1932, with his uncle's encouragement, Stanley Bray decided to try to emulate Frank Sangorski's peacock masterpiece, working from the original drawings which had taken eight months to produce. Although the drawings were complete, surprisingly there was no record of the colour of the leathers originally used; this had less effect than might be imagined, because the decorations and tooling between them were so extensive that the coloured leather beneath was only visible on the spine and board edges. Bray actually used green instead of brown for the basic colour, but apart from that his work was close to Sangorski's dream. The binding took him seven years of what little spare time he had because of the amount of intricate detail involved. As an example, the mass of flowing lines necessitated the use of a gouge, which has a curved edge and consequently has to be used with extreme precision when working to measurements of one-thousandth of an inch if the line is to flow, without revealing the joins. The boards on which the leather was mounted were three deep, and Bray wore out six dozen fretsaws in cutting his sunk panels.

Completion coincided with the outbreak of World

The Omar Khayyam. The photographs of 1912 cannot do justice to Sangorski & Sutcliffe's masterpiece lost with the Titanic. The 1,051 jewels incorporated in the outer covers and the doublures included topaz in the cascading peacock tails, turquoises in the crowns. The outer border of vineleaves is filled with amethyst grapes. Apart from the mass of intricate tooling, most of the decoration is onlaid leather, much of it paper-thin. Five thousand separate pieces of leather made it a kaleidoscope of colour. The doublures are just as detailed: the front with its hypnotically real snake (its eye a real emerald) symbolising Life, and the skull at the back, Death. If somehow miraculously resurrected intact, the Omar today would be priceless.

War II, and Bray sent his creation to a special depository for safe keeping. In 1941, in one of the worst of London's air-raids, the depository was hit, and the binding – encased in a lead-lined strong-box – was destroyed. Ironically, the protected pages remained intact, somewhat charred at the edges, but the leather with its fine decoration was baked, although the jewels survived (except the turquoises, which turned black). The irony is that had the binding stayed in the firm's workshop, it would have survived. Sangorski & Sutcliffe have received many offers to try again, but although Stanley Bray has prepared the ground, the task has to date proved too daunting. It seems unlikely that anyone could now be found with the skill, and the *time*.

Stanley Bray spent the war years on more mundane activities, such as supervising the manufacture of a million banana-shaped leather bands for the inside of

This Dickens scene is typical of the 'Kelliegram' bindings, by Kelly & Son, London, of the 1920s. *(Charles J. Sawyer)*

"TAKE THIS LITTLE VILLAIN AWAY" SAID THE AGONISED MR. PICKWICK.

steel helmets. There was also 'war work' of a more prestigious nature: George Sutcliffe, shortly before his death, furnished the crimson and gold-tooled leather scabbard of the Stalingrad Sword.

The third survivor at the top of the bookbinding market is George Bayntun of Bath, Avon – site of a Museum of Bookbinding opened in 1977 – although today the company is better known in bookselling circles than for its fine binding. George Bayntun started the binding operation in 1894, initially binding books and magazines for private or trade customers. He soon realised it was more profitable to buy books and re-sell them after re-covering or restoring, and took on London binders to raise the standard of craftsmanship. Establishing a reputation for good work at low prices, he took over several small binderies on the retirement of their owners, and in 1939 moved into the first division with the acquisition of one of the great names, Robert Rivière & Son, which had moved to London from Bath in 1840. This brought the vast collection of Rivière hand tools and plant into use again.

In addition to running his bindery and bookshops (he was appointed Bookseller to Her Majesty, Queen Mary shortly before his death at the beginning of World War II), George Bayntun published sets of Surtees' sporting novels, the engravings hand-coloured by local women; Ingpen's edition of Boswell's *Life of Johnson*, lavishly illustrated; and other major works. The business flagged after his death but was rejuvenated and expanded by his grandson, Hylton Bayntun-Coward who took over in 1963 and was President of the Antiquarian Booksellers Association in 1980–2.

The mainstay of the business for so long, through its bookselling connections, had been sets of half and even quarter bindings of popular authors, such as Dickens, Kipling, Austen and the Brontës. In the past ten years because of the changes in the market, the emphasis has been on smaller runs and more elaborate finishing. Among the recent special bindings have been books for presentation to, for example, the former United States ambassador to Britain, Walter Annenburg, who received Burke's *Lives of the American Presidents*, bound in full red morocco with a miniature of George Washington, under glass, in the front cover. Another was a book on the Houses of Parliament presented by the Speaker of the House of Commons to President Reagan when he visited the Palace of Westminster in 1982. The book was in full green morocco tooled in a gothic design in keeping with the building, and with pieces of the original wallpaper of the Lords and Commons used for the end-papers.

The distinguished London bindery W. T. Morrell,

(right) Occasionally Philip Smith displays his talent as a painter with books he feels can best be captured illustratively and symbolically. For *The Romaunt of the Rose*, by Geoffrey Chaucer and Guillaume de Lorris (printed in two columns, Old English alongside Old French), in a modern edition, he has set his paintings against a background of dark pink French morocco inlaid with rectangular panels of dark blue oasis on which he has also used maril as a decoration. On the front cover, slightly inset, he has used acrylic pigments on handmade paper to depict the walled garden of the story, which magically becomes as big as the world once entered. On the wall below are maril images of characters inside: envy, despair, etc. The area of blue sky at the top takes the shape of a bird in flight. The lower cover depicts spiritual love in the guise of a rose against the union of lovers.

(below right) It has been said that design was not Douglas Cockerell's forte, but his decoration of this *Facsimile of the MS of Milton's Minor Poems* (1904) is stunning. A large book (375 × 287 × 30mm), the feature is of course the gold tooling, an all-over design of roses and leaves. On the back cover (in the place of John Milton) are the dates 1608 : 1674. From the Broxbourne Library collection. *(The Bodleian Library)*

(overleaf) Philip Smith's binding of *Hamlet* is an expressive interpretation of the drama in psychological terms. The front board is divided geometrically along classical lines by the letters HAM above and LET below, containing elements and incidents found in the play; eg the whole cover is the face of Hamlet, with the ship carrying the Prince of England as his 'eye' (which symbolises also Hamlet's moment of insight into the plot against him while on board ship). The group of figures carrying off Hamlet's body form his mouth. The points of the crown, in which the letter A contains Ophelia (his conscience), strike down like a ray of light from above, and, across the covers, shape into the towers and battlements of Elsinore castle. His father's ghost hovers between Heaven (the church quatrefoil window) and Hell (red flames) on the spine of the book, pointing to the inset depicting the pernicious usurping royal couple. The mad Ophelia is drowned below. Other details in the leather fragments are Yorick's skull, masks of the players, the poison goblet and the thorns of life.

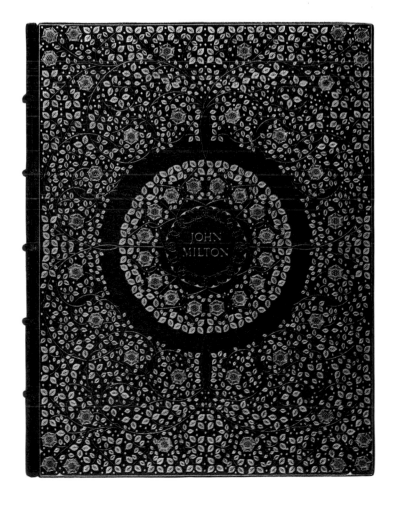

founded in 1860 and at one time employing around 100 skilled craftsmen, finally closed in 1983. Its last major work was a limited edition (295 copies) of Meinertzhagen's *The Birds of Arabia*. Ten special copies featured a resplendent bird of prey onlaid in coloured leathers – but ironically Morrell's had to subcontract that to a specialist firm.

One traditional operation has an assured future, however – the British Library bindery, largest in the world and, despite cutbacks, still employing over 120 skilled craftsmen. Economic problems are an important consideration here too, but are not caused by the shortage of orders; there is a never-ending stream of material needing attention. It is simply that the size of the workload strains the Library's budget to its limits, so that – as in so many crafts – it is difficult to attract and keep men and women of the right calibre; despite the long and expensive training, they could earn more in many non-skilled activities.

Most of the British Library bindery's work is repair and conservation. Not only is the hectic routine there fascinating in its own right – the research and development team leads the world in this work – but also its craftsmen can produce some very special individual bindings when an occasion demands. Most of them are employed in workshops in the vast British Museum complex, but others work at the lesser-known House of Lords Library (a relic of the days when the bindery was controlled by Her Majesty's Stationery Office, the government printers), and the newspaper library at Colindale. Because of the nature of their work there is an even greater need for specialisation, but this happens only after a thorough training programme; at one time recruits took a seven-year apprenticeship before setting foot in the building; today it still takes four years to qualify to the required standard. After a further grounding in the Library's special requirements – which can range from the repair of a first folio Shakespeare to the simple binding of magazines – these men and women are channelled into three main areas of specialisation: conservation and restoration, forwarding and finishing.

The Library believes that not even the most brilliant hand binder working alone can match the combination of talents achieved by the best of these specialists who – when they are that good – are capable of working as one unit. The Library's binding activities are sometimes criticised, because the range of demands placed on it diminish the relative importance of the binding role; the restoration of the contents of a book may be considered more important than the cover. Roy

Edgar Mansfield's binding for *The Duchess of Malfi*.

Although known as 'Cosway' bindings because of the painted miniatures inlaid on leather, many of those that appeared between 1912 and 1940 were the work of the miniaturist Miss C. B. Currie. In this binding (by Rivière) the portrait of Robert Burns was set in the doublure. *(Charles J. Sawyer)*

Russell, manager of the bindery since 1977, concedes that because of budgetary restrictions his prime task has to be the availability of works of reference to the Library's users. If, for example, it is particularly costly to repair a book of manuscripts, then it makes sense to save on the binding by using a simple but durable half-leather or buckram, knowing that it is functional but not an aesthetic masterpiece. On the other hand, because of the tremendous collection of tools available for decorating purposes, elaborate designs can be reproduced down to the last detail. When a binding is damaged beyond repair or lost completely, no attempt is made to guess at what it might have been.

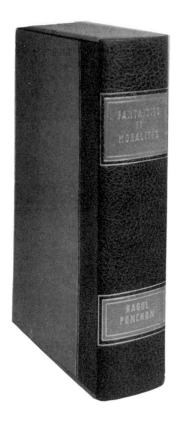

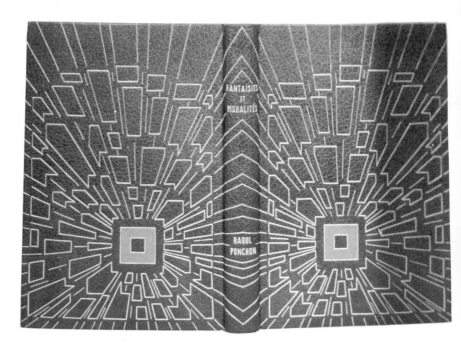

Fantasies et Moralities, by Raoul Ponchon, designed and bound by apprentices at the British Library bindery. Yellow tooling and inlays on black. *(British Library bindery)*

Technicians at the bindery were the first in the world to develop the ability to remove harmful acids from paper, which has changed the face of conservation, working with William J. Barrow, the American conservator who came up with the original mathematical calculations. These skills are one of the reasons why the British Library is probably the only national library where the student is, whenever possible, allowed access to original material instead of photostats. Every effort is made to 'stabilise' original books and manuscripts (not just in paper and leather but in other materials, for example linen), for constant availability – instead of locking them away in the hope of repairs at some future time when money or improved technology might be available. (Even other important institutions such as the magnificent Library of Congress in Washington cannot offer the same service in this respect.)

For these meticulous craftsmen there is little scope for creativity; but from time to time the bindery is asked to produce presentation books for special occasions, often for Royalty. Until recently, on completion of their apprenticeship the craftsmen would prepare a special binding for presentation to the Library, and some of that work matches the standards of many 'name' binders. Among the Library's millions of books is a textbook about the work of the great French binder Pierre Legrain. A student handling it today might imagine the binding was designed by the master himself, and therefore worth a small fortune. It was not; it is the work of a former apprentice.

3

THE INDIVIDUAL COMES INTO HIS OWN

Talented newcomers were encouraged to follow Cobden-Sanderson's lead in exploring the craft's full potential, and not merely to copy what had gone before. It was his pupil Douglas Bennett Cockerell (1870–1945) who provided the necessary continuity and who was to play a major part in the development of bookbinding over the next four decades – through his own work, his flair for teaching and inspiring others and through the message expounded to a much wider public in his *Bookbinding and The Care of Books* (1901), which became a standard work, running to many editions.

It is not uncommon for people to discover their true talent by accident; Cockerell's good fortune was that his brother Sydney was secretary of William Morris's Kelmscott Press, which led to a meeting with Cobden-Sanderson. On the death of their father, Douglas went to Canada at the age of fifteen to make his fortune. It was tough for a period; working as a farm boy, a junior in a bank, and then becoming manager of a branch in the Far West where the type of clientele meant that he needed a revolver in his desk drawer. Returning to England for a visit, he decided to stay.

He was still only twenty-three when he became an apprentice at the Doves Bindery, but within four years he was sufficiently qualified to take a bookbinding class at the newly established Central School of Arts & Crafts, run by the London County Council (remaining an instructor there for forty years), and a year later set up in business on his own. From 1905 to 1915 he was manager of the highly regarded W. H. Smith & Son bindery, which he had merged with his own, before again going independent (with his son, Sydney). During the war he worked in a supervisory capacity in munitions, and in 1918 was awarded the MBE for his industry. In later years he taught at the Royal College of Art, and lectured annually to students of librarianship at University College, London – the material from this led to the publication in 1929 of his *Some Notes on Bookbinding*.

The new partnership operating from the Cockerell home provided greater scope for demonstrating his convictions about integrity in binding; materials must be suitable and chemically sound, and the rule must be to do what was best for the book, which was not necessarily the same as suiting the whim of a collector. Also he could encourage his son in reviving the use of vellum for fine binding, and the introduction of new methods and tools. As a measure of the changing balance between traditional trade binders and the new wave, epitomised by him and his pupils, Douglas Cockerell was invited by the British Museum in 1935 to rebind its recently acquired *Codex Sinaiticus*, the fourth-century Greek manuscript of the bible, of such importance that it is still on public display fifty years later.

Cockerell brought respectability to the new wave of private binders by the quality of his work and his constant campaigning for higher standards. He was concerned not just with the finished product; he was instrumental (with Cobden-Sanderson) in setting up a Society of Arts committee on leather reform – long overdue because of the way standards had deteriorated. An interesting analogy was presented by Bernard C. Middleton, historian of bookbinding techniques and a former President of Designer Bookbinders, in an article in the Private Libraries Association journal in 1981:

There is a tendency for old buildings in streets lined with shops gradually to lose their character by the replacement of damaged features with somewhat unsuitable ones, and for accretions gradually to obliterate the basic period structure, but so gradually that everyone has forgotten what the buildings were like and unthinkingly accepts the mess. The same kind of thing happened in bookbinding. The rot had set in much earlier, but in the 1860s, 70s and 80s the structure of some bindings was nothing short of ludicrous, especially in the case of large family bibles pretentiously got up with heavy brass fittings on

extremely thick bevelled boards pathetically inadequately attached to the book with a few thin cords, and stuck-in cloth inner joints. The essential character of the book itself was often lost because the edge gilding, especially on the concave fore-edges, was so perfect that the effect was more like a solid block of gold than a collection of paper leaves. Leather was denaturised by excessive paring, pressing and artificial graining, marbling and hard polishing. Cockerell tried to set new standards in his 'Specification For Bookbinding' and pointed out that if the lacing-in showed a little it was not unsightly and indeed made a good starting point for decoration . . .

Mistaken priorities, and insensitive treatment, such as the unnatural-looking 'polish' to which Middleton refers, were constantly in Cockerell's mind. In his *Some Notes on Bookbinding*, dealing with the proper way of judging a binding, he writes: 'A too hard, machine-like appearance can result from misapplied skill. A fine binding should in the first place be judged by its appearance, and can then be examined in detail . . .' He warns of complacency.

I regard myself as a hand binder, and have the greatest possible regard for handwork directed by the brain, but I have no respect whatever for handwork merely because it is done by hand . . . I am expecting some day to be offered a glass of water with the recommendation that it is real hand-pumped . . . You can by using poor materials and faulty methods make very bad bindings by machinery. But from equally faulty materials and methods just as bad bindings can be . . . and are produced by hand.

The rift between trade binders and individuals was widening, the former regarding the latter as amateurs who had no right to be laying down the law — a complaint that was too often justified. Unfortunately, there was to be no reconciliation — there is resentment even today, when most of the criticisms on both sides are no longer valid. The seeds fell on stony ground, and with notable exceptions (such as Sangorski & Sutcliffe who had been Cockerell's pupils) the trade binders became increasingly introverted. In the main they did what was easiest — what had been done before — and so they repeated the 'successes' of a hundred years earlier.

Because of the impact of his strong views on

A delightfully simple design by Douglas Cockerell for Apuleius', *De Cupidinis et Psyches Amoribus* was forwarded and tooled by his son Sydney in 1927. The binding is in green morocco; gold-tooled single-line knot with red onlay centres to the small circles. (*Victoria & Albert Museum*)

structure and techniques (which included the introduction of different materials, such as tawed — alum-dressed — pigskin, which was likely to outlast all vegetable-tanned leathers), it is easy to play down Douglas Cockerell's design skills. He was not a brilliant designer, but he sparked off an *art nouveau* style that was extensively copied. Using 'intaglio' blind tooling very effectively, his decorations tended (like Cobden-Sanderson's) to feature plant forms, but were far more expansive in the area covered, and most were distinctive. The respected veteran binder Roger Powell, another of Cockerell's pupils and himself a successful teacher, recalls that at one stage the 'master' would complain that all bindings looked the same (as his!). The question of 'subconscious' copying is a fascinating one; there are certain similarities in some of his designs — at least in those featuring plain oval shapes — and in the work of men who would never have consciously copied him, the Frenchmen Pierre Legrain and Paul Bonet.

Incidentally, Cobden-Sanderson was not alone in encouraging the talents of 'outsiders'. In 1898 the Guild of Women Binders had been formed, and within five years its membership had grown to forty, but without the guidance of anyone of Cobden-Sanderson's stature the quality of their work was uneven, and the Guild was soon liquidated. The Hampstead Bindery, predominantly for men, was also started in 1898 and employed some talented professional binders, but that too was shortlived. Because of the economic pressures of the 1920s and 1930s men left the West End binderies to find security elsewhere — in most cases to the British Museum bindery, where the work was of high quality but traditional and lacking in creativity. The opportunities for individuals to make their names remained limited, and those that did had to have some special quality.

In a trade where long apprenticeships were deemed essential, and the new school of hand binders were invariably dismissed as amateurs, it is interesting to reflect on the skill of Katharine Adams (1862–1952), whose work is admired today for its technical competence, yet was carried out after a training that lasted only four months. She built on a natural aptitude and learned from experience. At the age of eighty-eight, Roger Powell claims that he is still learning, still encountering new problems and is still kept awake at night worrying how he will tackle certain features of the job in hand.

Born in a time and social class when women did not need to earn a living, Katharine Adams was exposed to the artistic influence of the William Morris circle; her father had been to school and university with him, and

A LITTLE BOOK OF LIFE & DEATH

1910

I SOMETIMES THINK MY HEAVEN MAY BE A GREEN PLACE, WITH AN ORCHARD TREE, AND ONE SWEET ANGEL, KNOWN TO ME.

as a child she would play with Morris's two daughters. Binding was something to which she took instinctively; indeed her first commission came from Mrs Morris. Her formal training consisted of three months under Sarah Prideaux, a disciple of Morris, and one month under Douglas Cockerell. Apart from the technical skill she acquired, she is considered to be one of the few binders of any period who was effective in using gold for pictorial designs on leather.

In the Broxbourne collection in the Bodleian Library there is a charming little binding of Walter Pater's *An Imaginary Portrait* (Daniel Press 1894, limited to 250 copies), which Katharine Adams (Mrs Webb) completed in 1916, and inside is her invoice for 3 guineas (£3.15). The book, which Mr Ehrman had obtained in 1939 in exchange for another binding, has a gold-tooled monogram on the front and an oak tree on the lower in pointillé style. In a letter to her customer she wrote on 7 November 1916: 'The effect of the dotted background was quite intentional. The effect of light on the gold can be varied by the angle at which the tool is used. That background was worked with the book upside down – if you turn it you will see the difference.' Almost seventy years later I did as she suggested, and can confirm that she was right, although I have not reproduced the book here because the effect is lost in a photograph. In a letter to Mr Ehrman in 1947 – at the age of eighty-five – she reported working on what was probably her last binding. '. . . and I am not quite sure I can see well enough perhaps to finish it.'

More of a trendsetter although less competent as a binder was Sybil Pye, who started binding in 1906 with no formal training at all – claiming that she learned everything from reading *Bookbinding & The Care of Books*. Her critics, in the main craft-orientated, claim that her forwarding was so bad ('it would fall to pieces as soon as you looked at it') that she could not possibly have read Cockerell's book – or at least not properly! But her many more admirers maintain that she was the most important woman binder of her age because of the freshness she brought to cover design, and the bold style in which she finished her work. Most of the bindings are based on inlays of different-colour leathers – frequently strong shades of blue or mauve and green – though at this time decoration other than tooling was usually *on*lay work (pieces of leather were placed on top, as opposed to being cut into the cover).

Katharine Adams bound *A Little Book of Life and Death*, edited by Elizabeth Waterhouse, in 1925. The design is in gold tooling on brown levant morocco. On the lower cover, interesting single gold lines form a pattern of eight rows of five squares, with a single gold dot in each corner. From the Broxbourne Library collection. *(The Bodleian Library)*

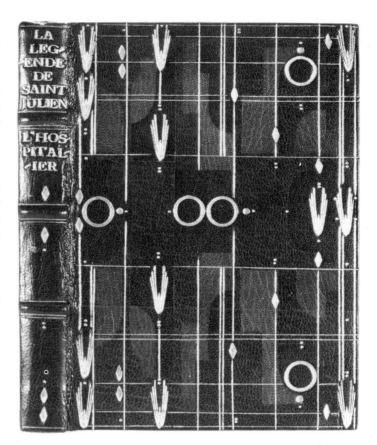

Typical of Sybil Pye's distinctive style – a 1926 binding of Flaubert's *Le Legende de Saint Julien l'Hospitalier*. Black morocco, inlaid with blue and green and tooled in gold. *(Victoria & Albert Museum)*

A craftsman has to allow for shrinkage, so that cutting and filling the 'holes' is a precision business; at one time craftsmen had insured against mistakes by concealing the leather joins with gold tooling.

These days, inlay is taken so much for granted that the work of such binders as Philip Smith who lean towards 'busy' canvases with remarkable detail, could pass for paintings; but it was considered a risk in Sybil Pye's time. Yet apart from slight fading to the strong colours (on the exposed side), the bindings remain as fresh as new forty and fifty years later. The distinctive style, combining linear tooling with geometric shapes, considered uncharacteristically masculine, is not so much a design as (to quote Sybil Pye) 'a pattern suggested by the colour and surface in the leathers themselves'.

Meanwhile, on the Continent, the French (and to a lesser extent the Germans, led by Franz Weisse of Hamburg) were reasserting their supremacy (which many Parisians would insist they had never lost), revitalised by one of the outstanding figures of the century, Pierre Legrain. Trained as a cabinetmaker and designer (another example of the close link between craftsmen in leather and wood), Legrain was asked in 1917 to design a few book covers for a collector. From the start he revealed a talent not only for capturing on leather the spirit of contemporary trends in art — perhaps the first binder consciously to relate the craft with art — but to adapt it to the subject of the book he was binding. Edgar Mansfield who had many ideas in common with Legrain, later said of him: 'It wasn't enough for him to make patterns with the tools he had on hand, which might have been just as suitable for carpets or wallpaper designs, but to attempt designs which express the essence of the book in that ornamentation.'

One of the most significant features of Legrain's work was to recognise the book shape as being three-dimensional instead of seeing it as two panels and spine, and therefore to allow his designs to flow off the edges of the covers. Hitherto, binders had experimented within the traditional framework with symmetrical and usually floral or arabesque panels. What is remarkable is that Legrain's influence is still felt today, yet he was active for little more than ten

Donald Glaister, of California, paid tribute to Pierre Legrain with this design, featuring the use of circles, the basis of so many of the designs by the French master (for instance, see photograph on page 92).

A Treatyse of Fysshynge With An Angle, by Dame Juliana, was bound by Charles McLeish Jnr in 1950. The simple but striking design of gold tooling is set against a bold green background. From the Broxbourne Library collection. *(The Bodleian Library)*

years, until his death in 1929; most 'name' binders have had decades to develop their reputations.

Legrain's mantle was taken on by Paul Bonet, even more revered in some circles, and whose influence as a designer was uninhibited by his limitations as a craftsman — an issue to which we return later. Bonet's only previous experience was in fashion designing, which appears to have little in common with design on leather. Meanwhile, it is significant that for all their sophistication in design, the technical accomplishment of the French hand binders did not compare with that of their English contemporaries. Though in demand, for their artistic merit, French bindings were treated with some caution by many international collectors. Major J. R. Abbey, whose enormous collection included the work of many French binders, is on record as asking friends not to handle them, because they did not open properly. (A party trick of some of the older British binders is to turn a book inside-out, and holding the covers by their ends shake the contents vigorously to demonstrate how soundly constructed it is.)

In England for a long period, the private presses provided opportunities for the best binders to work

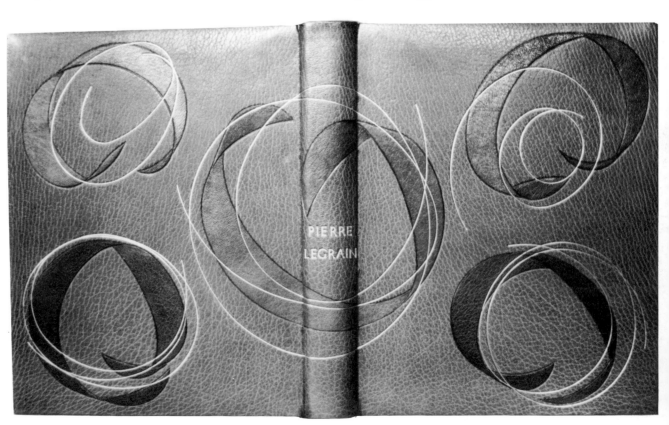

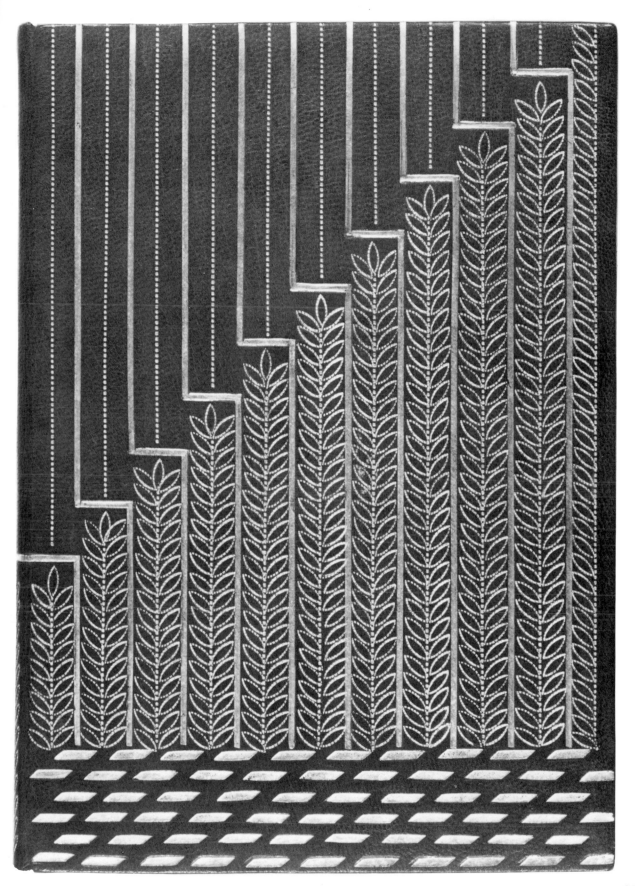

without restrictions. Up to twenty-five copies of each title would be specially bound and these would sometimes represent very fine craftsmanship. Perhaps the best examples were the Ashendene Press (1894–1935), run by C. H. St John Hornby, a man of vision but better known in the printing trade, and later the Gregynog Press (1922–40, relaunched in 1978), the outstanding source of fine bindings between the two wars.

Not many private presses could justify the expense of a full-time binder, but Ashendene was fortunate in that St John Hornby was also a director of the W. H. Smith bindery – in its best years supervised by Douglas Cockerell, who had merged it with his own firm until he began again in a smaller way with his son. Another, Katharine Adams, was a personal friend. In later years commissions were given to the best hand binders available. My favourite binding of an Ashendene Press book was one of 150 copies which Charles McLeish did as late as 1950. Born in Edinburgh in 1886, he came to London four years later when his father, also Charles, went to work for Rivière & Son. It was when he joined Cobden-Sanderson on the formation of the Doves Bindery that he was able to fulfil his promise; Rivière produced superb work but always traditional in design and often repetitive. Young Charles was apprenticed to a small but distinguished firm, Roger de Coverly, but in 1909 father and son went into partnership as C. & C. McLeish. They were not short of work, and among their first customers was the Doves Bindery. Like so many craftsmen, it was not until his middle years when he had gained confidence that some of McLeish's best work was done.

The Gregynog Press could merit a chapter in its own right because of the consistently high level of publishing it maintained for twenty years, during which its bindings set the standards for craftsmen everywhere – except perhaps France, where the influence of Legrain and Bonet had transformed the binding scene. Named after the property in which it is housed in Powys, Wales, the Press was founded by the sisters Gwendoline and Margaret Davies, whose grandfather David Davies (1818–90) was one of the great industrial entrepreneurs of the nineteenth century. Originally, it was their intention to make Gregynog into an arts and crafts centre for Wales; the dream was not fulfilled, but one of the results was the formation of a fine printing press. From 1923 to 1940 it produced forty-two books in limited edition, most of them bound by a brilliant staff binder, George Fisher, who ironically had accepted his initial appointment with reluctance.

Another former pupil of Douglas Cockerell, Fisher had learned forwarding with an amateur binder and

finishing as an apprentice with Rivière & Son, but he found it difficult to make a living and bought a 5 acre smallholding in 1911. When Gregynog decided to employ a binder in 1925, Douglas Cockerell recommended Fisher, although he may not have realised that his former pupil had done no binding for ten years. Fisher accepted the proposal of one month's trial but when the job was offered to him he was undecided because of having to give up the farm; he asked for a wage he thought would be outside Gregynog's budget, but – to his surprise – it was agreed. He stayed with the Press until its demise in World War II.

In keeping with the policy of the Press, most of the designs for George Fisher's binders were the work of its talented small staff of engravers and illustrators, although he was capable of providing his own designs, and occasionally did. He is associated mainly with the designs of Blair Hughes-Stanton and the partnership obviously worked. Yet he told Dorothy Harrop, the bookbinding historian, and author of a history of the Gregynog Press, that he considered many to be more suited to the printed page than tooled leather: 'They interested me more than they pleased me.' As already mentioned, in the context of Paul Bonet, the relationship between designers and binders is much debated, but Fisher demonstrated that partnerships can be profitable, provided the designer is able to give the binder his head, and not the other way about. Another of Gregynog's most interesting bindings (of the first twenty-five copies) was Robert Vansittart's *The Singing Caravan*, on which the cover decoration was the creation of William McCance, a Scottish painter and sculptor (whose wife, the wood-engraver Agnes Miller Parker, also did work for the Press). Admitting his lack of knowledge as to what was feasible on leather, McCance merely provided a rough charcoal sketch from which Fisher had to complete the design and produce his binding.

Three very different designs bound by George Fisher at the Gregynog Press.

The Lamentations of Jeremiah, 1934, features a design by his most frequent collaborator, Blair Hughes-Stanton. Worked on black levant morocco, a disc in blue oasis onlaid adjoins an area of blind and heavy gilt lines. The sword hanging from the disc is tooled in gilt and blind; the six squares onlaid in white and outlined in gilt. *(National Library of Wales)*

The Singing Caravan, by Robert Vansittart, was designed by William McCance, although Fisher had to interpret a rough charcoal sketch for this binding in orange oasis in 1932. *(National Library of Wales)*

Shaw Gives Himself Away was designed by Paul Nash and bound in 1939. The morocco is dark green and the onlays orange. *(Victoria & Albert Museum)*

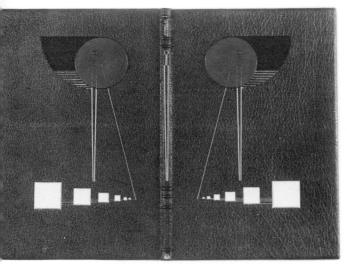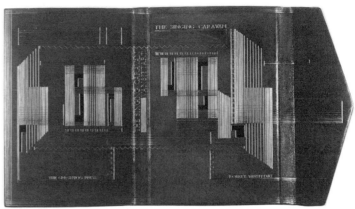

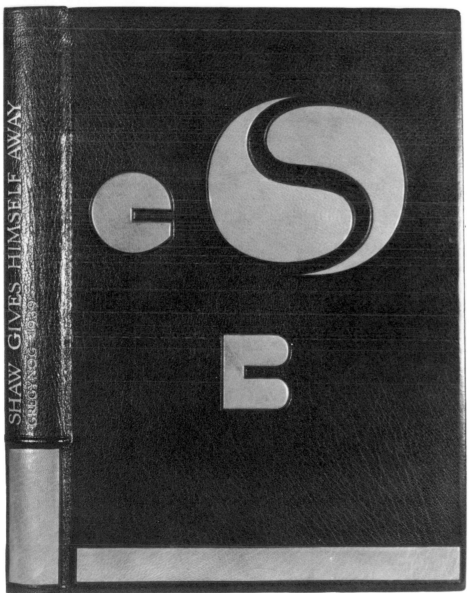

We are all, of course, prisoners of our age; just as sportsmen of the 1930s had the misfortune of being born a half-century too early, so craftsmen of the same period were never properly recompensed for their talent. Gifted hand binders like Fisher and McLeish were happy to earn modest payment for work that in today's climate (given appropriate media publicity) would often fetch hundreds and even thousands of pounds or dollars. Perhaps the binder best exemplifying this disparity in values was William Matthews (1898–1977), another remembered primarily as a teacher (his most famous pupil was Edgar Mansfield), but who was also a superb craft binder and, unusually for his background, a very original designer – in the sense of the variety of his work. Most of his best bindings were for London's West End antiquarian booksellers, who had always been the principal support of the trade; it ranged from traditional, adapted to current requirements, to exciting modern styles – many in his later years incredibly fresh for someone of his maturity.

Matthews had worked with W. T. Morrell, then at the height of their success, as an apprentice finisher. He left to join the army in World War I, but returned in 1919 to complete his apprenticeship. In 1923 he began to explore his potential as a teacher, going back to the Central School, to which he had won a scholarship when a boy. Here he continued to take evening classes for forty years – and other students during the day – although in that time he taught at a number of schools and polytechnics in the Home Counties. Another of the talented craftsmen who designed and cut his own tools, Matthews anticipated the modern movement by regarding the binding as being not merely decorative covers but related, in a subordinate role, to the author's work. The relationship did not always have to be illustrative, although when it was, the result – for example the daisy pattern for W. G. Davie's *Old Cottages and Farmhouses in Surrey*, bound in 1935, was dazzlingly simple.

As the dozen or so outstanding binders of the first half of the century brought such different qualities to the craft, it is difficult to compare them in terms of status. But since I have already singled out Cobden-Sanderson and Douglas Cockerell as men of special standing, that line of development may be worth continuing. It is generally conceded that Edgar Mansfield changed the face of cover design more than anyone before or since. He was the first creative artist (as opposed to craftsman) to bring 'outside' talents to binding, and his impact on the medium was by what he did, and by the ideas he passed on to others.

Born in London in 1907, he grew up in New Zealand, where he studied art. As a teacher his interest extended to applied crafts and pottery, and because he felt that New Zealand was more naturally a crafts country, but lacked teachers with the right training, he returned to England, at the age of twenty-seven, to get that experience himself. At the Central School and the Camberwell School of Art, he began with pottery, then added fabric printing, and finally bookbinding (under William Matthews) for the next five years, at Central School and privately. They developed a great affinity.

Mansfield recalls:

The crafts were no problem because these were taught by highly skilled and practising craftsmen. Creative design was another matter, until in 1935 the Reimann School of Industrial Design came to London from Berlin, and for the first time I met teachers who appreciated modern Art and knew what the creative act was about.

The school was partly for teaching and partly an industrial design centre accepting commissions for various projects. The teachers were all expert professionals and were not infrequently changed when one happened to be employed on a commission. I came to realise – a shock to a trained teacher – that an expert who couldn't teach would still be infinitely preferable to a teacher who didn't do. Experience has confirmed this opinion. So, under the influence of Elsa Taterka, who till the day she died could not speak English well, I found my own confidence and creative direction in design and art. I was forced to discover the logic – the reasons why – not from what she taught, because she didn't, as such, but from what she accepted and what she rejected. In the end I always gave her the reasons, and she thought I was very clever and had discovered them – or perhaps she didn't hear; she was also deaf.

Meanwhile, in bookbinding he quickly recognised the relationship between the rigid rectangular cover boards and the painting surface of a picture; the scope for line and coloured areas, for texture; and the basic theme arising from the contents. 'Thus it happened by chance,' he says, 'that I became the first modern creative artist and designer to train seriously as a bookbinder, with the inevitable result – my departure from the decorative and the illustrative towards the

William Matthews's reputation was earned by his craftsmanship, not design, yet most of his work vividly captured the mood of the book on which he was working, usually in illustrative terms but also symbolically. His 1961 binding for James Weale's *Bookbindings In the South Kensington Museum* (1898) features the elements of binding in a surprisingly modern design. (*Victoria & Albert Museum*)

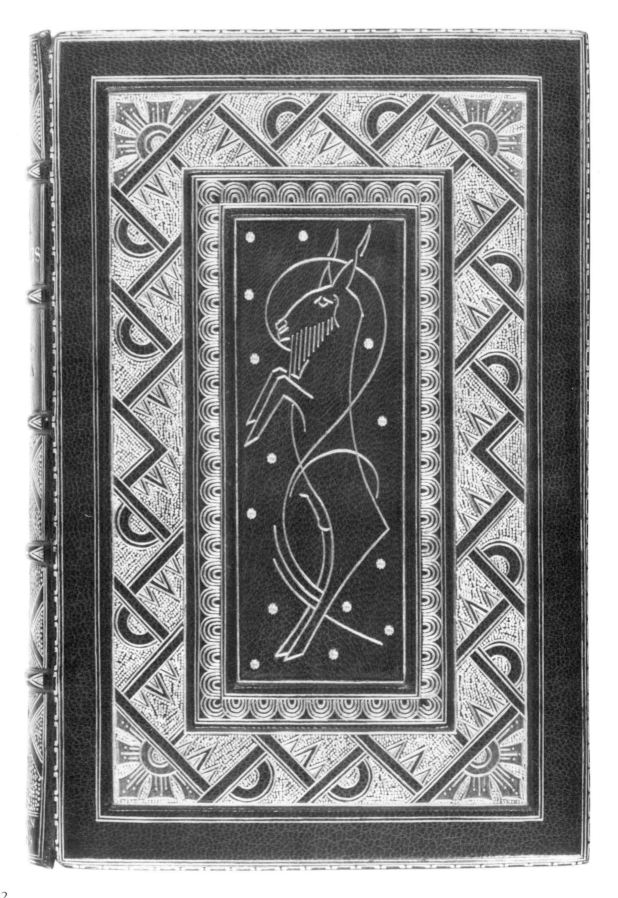

expressive and evocative met with strong opposition, then with tolerance, and finally with acceptance.'

Much of the opposition was from traditionalists who refused to accept the views of an outsider who, for all his instinctive talent, had not served his apprenticeship in acquiring some of the basic craft skills. It is true that he had no pretensions to being a first-class forwarder, but rumours that he was a designer who merely dabbled in binding and who allowed his tutor, William Matthews, to do much of his finishing are vehemently denied by several binders who watched him working alone, often in the presence of Matthews. The quality of his gilding for which he made most of his own finishing tools was also beyond dispute. A more valid criticism of him is *as* a designer – that because of his background in art, and the influence on him of painters, particularly French – he did not conceive the book as a three-dimensional form: his designs tended to relate to the front and back boards, and not the spine which defines the three dimensions. Ironically, a criticism of his widely admired sculpture is that it has a strong graphic influence. Despite any carping, Mansfield gave binding a great impetus through his ideas in design, and perhaps even more by his conviction that craftsmen had been taking the medium – leather – for granted for too long, and that its natural beauty was not sufficiently recognised. To make his point he startled the 'establishment' by innovations such as the use of blemishes as an expressive feature, and gathering or moulding the leather.

It was Mansfield's pottery that supplemented his income initially, and it was not until after the war (he was repatriated from the armed forces to New Zealand before returning to London in 1948) that the true originality of his work was appreciated, and even then by other countries before England. While teaching full-time at the London College of Printing he found time to produce his most interesting work, evolving from new ideas in the use of leather and tools, and from the drawing which provided the experimental research – what he called his 'adventure' in line, shape and space, colour and texture. Musical structure (form)

In vivid contrast to the previous binding is Matthews's *Ur of the Chaldees*, by Leonard Woolley, bound in 1955. It is in the Broxbourne Library collection, with a note from Matthews: 'The whole design was prompted by and built up on motifs and ornaments depicted on numerous objects found by Sir Leonard Woolley in the tombs at Ur. Special tools were cut by myself. The work involved was considerable.' The centre sunk panel on the front bears a tooled design in gold based on the biblical story of 'The Ram Caught In A Thicket'; a matching panel on the back has a tooled device representing a Chaldean vase. Sunken panels on the sides are inlaid and tooled with a 'strap' design, with close 'powdered' background. *(The Bodleian Library)*

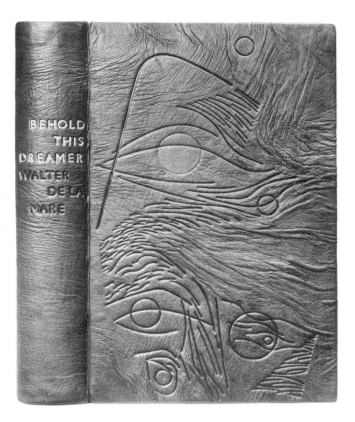

Edgar Mansfield's binding for *Behold This Dreamer (above)*: textures he has created in the leather enter the design, supplementing the tooling. *The Picture of Dorian Gray (below)* shows his use of inlay as well as tooling.

43

played an increasing role in the total integration — sonata form in particular. From 1949 every binding was reproduced in the German trade journal and frequently in similar journals in Switzerland, Holland and France.

In retrospect, time has a habit of making even momentous events seem like a brief diary entry, but Mansfield's struggle for originality must not be discounted. Objecting to many practices that obscured the natural beauty of the leather (particularly the grain), he encountered two barriers. The first was that bindings had 'always' been polished and varnished, if only as a means of protection against wear and insects, although today there are alternatives; the second was the traditional use of thinly pared leathers for ease in handling, and to save time. Mansfield defied these conventions in his efforts to exploit the expressive elasticity and richness of thicker leather. It is interesting to reflect on how much he may have been influenced (as was his design style) by French artists, such as Mannessier, because he once told me of the love of some of them for the 'juicy rich quality' of oil paint, and of the 'fluid translucence' of coloured water for others, while he described dry, neutral acrylic as 'something else'.

The emphasis of the grain was used on *Thirstland Treks*, to suggest the rugged landscape, and from then on he used the technique frequently to permit larger areas within the design to remain active, and to integrate them with the tooled and total area. He used thicker leather to retain the maximum grain quality, which thinner pared leathers lose, and also to permit deeper blind tooling — which gives more form to the lines and a greater feeling of full leather binding. He described the transition to me:

More and more I felt the original quality of the medium . . . goat skin, especially native dyed . . . but all. It offered the scope for a rich active surface, as also did the colour tone variations on native dyed skins, which the thinner or polished surfaces only hinted at. Later, I also inlaid strongly textured neck or other outer pieces from the skin, and even cut my cover from anywhere on the skin to exploit the best grained area, wasting the rest, except for use as inlays — which was absolute sacrilege to William Matthews and the others. In addition to using the fullest thickness practical, and emphasising the grain, I used full thickness leather for inlays, removing a little of the board underneath rather than paring the inlay to the required depth, or levelling in the polishing process. Without actually doing it, you can realise that thin leather pasted and applied, loses most of its texture because it lacks the strong thicker flesh

(right) Letters have always been a feature of Roger Powell's designs, as in this 1977 binding of Dürer's *The Just Shaping of Letters*.

(below right) Donald Glaister's interest in expressionist 'scribble' is shown by the gold tooling in this binding of *Wuthering Heights*. The design is inspired by his conception of Emily Brontë's story, in which the characters can never become masters of their own fates; they are controlled by a more powerful force, represented by vertical maroon lines, their configuration also influenced by the style of Clare Leighton's wood engravings inside the book.

(overleaf left) *The Rout of the Frost King*, a book of fairy tales by Neustadt published in 1908, is only 7 × 4in, and Lage Eric Carlson emphasised its size by setting it inside the sculptured head of the Frost King, covered in silver kid. The peaks of the crown become the tops of the trees on the inside covers, with the design encompassing the book itself.

(overleaf right) Ivor Robinson's mastery of gold tooling is illustrated by:
    Thucydides (1979), the helmet;
    Gospels (1983), the crucifixion.
Note the subtle use of colour.

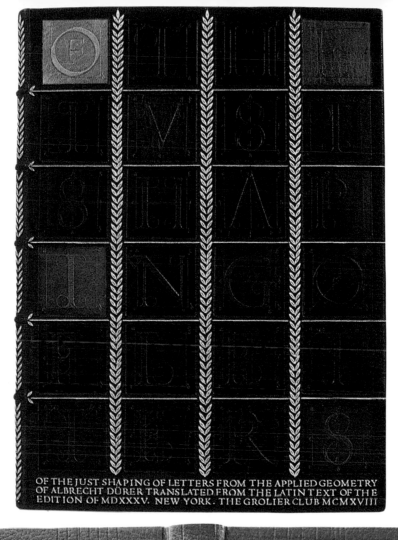

OF THE JUST SHAPING OF LETTERS FROM THE APPLIED GEOMETRY
OF ALBRECHT DÜRER TRANSLATED FROM THE LATIN TEXT OF THE
EDITION OF MDXXXV. NEW YORK. THE GROLIER CLUB MCMXVIII

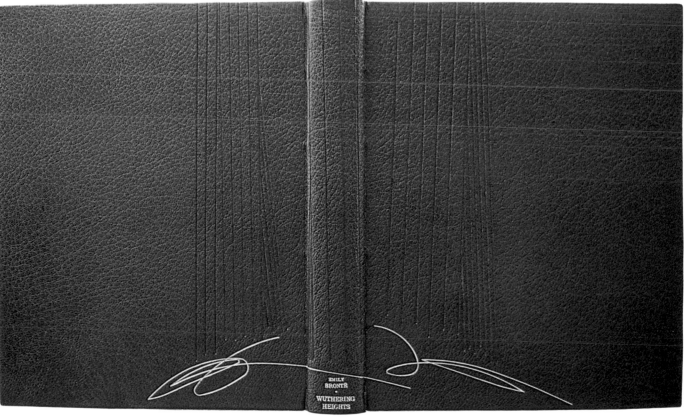

EMILY
BRONTË
*
WUTHERING
HEIGHTS

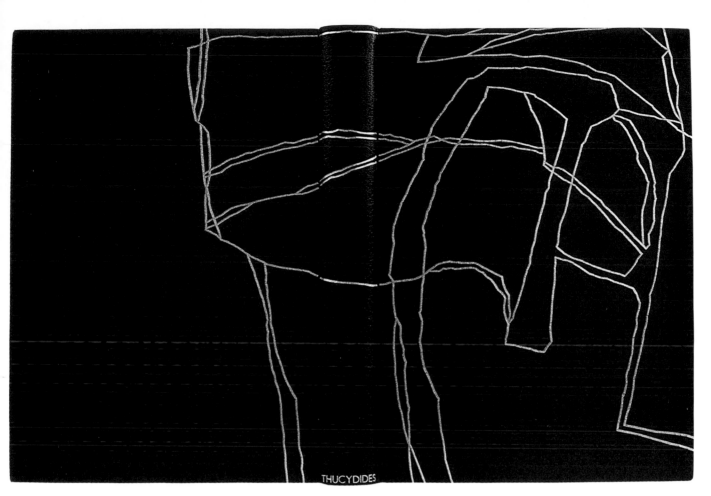

THUCYDIDES

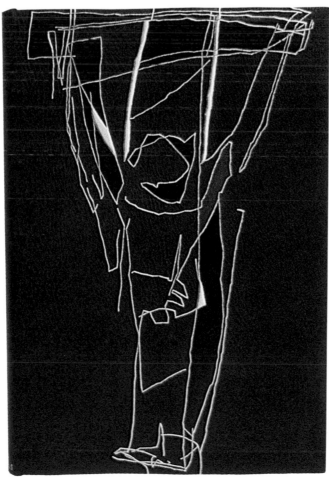

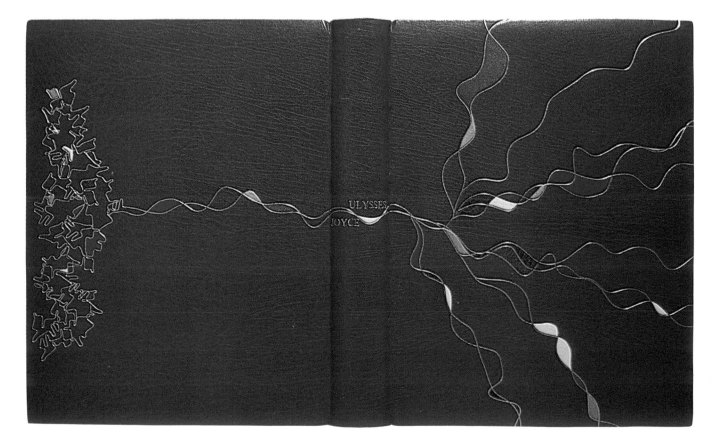

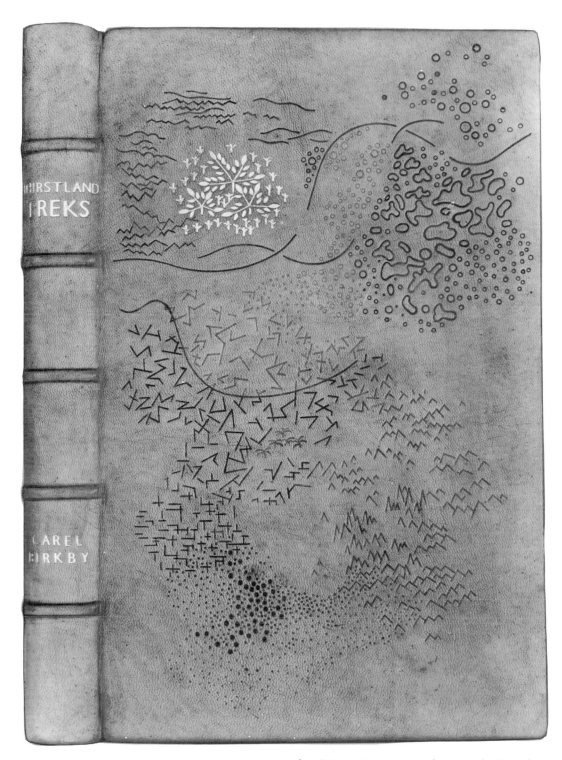

(above left) The inside of James Brockman's binding of *Beauty and Deformity* (see page 12).

(left) *Ulysses*: James Brockman created a striking effect by large and small wavy-line tools he made for himself. The design is built up by repeating the tooling in different combinations. The coloured leathers between the tooling are onlays.

(above) Most people associate Edgar Mansfield's work with abstract designs of great vitality; but it is his use of leather as an expressive medium in its own right that distanced him from other binders. *Thirstland Treks* by Carel Birkby, bound in 1948, was his first experiment in emphasising the grain – in this case to suggest a rugged landscape. 'I used the technique frequently to permit larger areas within the design to remain active and integrate with the tooled and total area, and used thicker leather to retain the maximum grain quality and permit deeper blind tooling.'

below (which is also its guts, its strength). Even so, I worked on a base of firm plastic to avoid the loss of grain working on a hard surface below while damp.

It was significant that, while Mansfield was aware of the new ideas appearing in France – and he admired the achievement of Pierre Legrain – he made no attempt to compete with them, and the French were quick to recognise the route he was taking. In his *The Book: Art & Object*, 1982, Philip Smith, arguably the outstanding binder of the past quarter-century and who elsewhere concedes his debt to Mansfield, writes:

He formed a preference for informal but tightly structured and controlled images, but combined this with the natural informality of certain leathers, mainly native dyed nigers, and natural grained Oasis . . . he was attracted by the organic looking and naturally blemished skins – usually rejected as second or third grade – and into these he worked additional stains and intensified the graining with slight wrinkling during the covering process. Critics considered this was an accident caused by unskilled covering. It might have occurred by clumsy handling by other, beginner bookbinders but Mansfield adopted it as a dynamic expressive feature. I suggest that this attitude to the organic was the master-stroke of Mansfield's originality and one which has contributed greatly to the later development of holistic book-art. It was something which no binder before him had considered of creative worth, but in fact we have here the seeds which were to germinate and diversify in the styles of present-day binders, and which link up with two present-day attitudes: the psychological and visual interpretation or extension of a particular thematic concept found in a book, and the concept of a book as a 'free-standing art object'. It also took bookbinding art a step closer to the day when it will be recognised and accepted as a pure art medium.

From 1964 Mansfield, feeling that he had nothing more to add to the medium, concentrated on his first loves – line drawing and sculpture – which had been developing since before 1950 (in 1980 he was to be elected Fellow of the Royal Society of British Sculptors). Only a few more bindings were produced, but almost 100 exhibition bindings are today housed in museums and private collections all over the world. His first honour in 1950, significantly, was to be elected first foreign member of the German bookbinders' guild (MDE). Five years later when the first similar British body, the Guild of Contemporary Bookbinders, was formed, he was elected its first president. In 1979 he was awarded the OBE for services to bookbinding and sculpture, and it would seem a strange oversight if he were not similarly honoured by New Zealand where he currently spends six months of the year – especially as in 1974 it was that government which asked him to bind a special edition of *The Life of Captain James Cook* to be New Zealand's wedding present to Princess Anne.

While Mansfield brought a stream of fresh air into creative work, there was less scope for innovation in the trade at large; the craft had, after all, taken hundreds of years to evolve and technically there was little room for refinements. Fortunately, there have always been men prepared to experiment and search for better answers. One of these was Thomas Harrison (1876–1955), who was a particularly skilful finisher, although that did not stop him looking at the structure of the binding. Apprenticed to one of the best firms outside London, Fazakerly of Liverpool, Harrison went on to become manager of Zaehnsdorf. Considered by many respected authorities – including Bernard Middleton, who remembers his singleminded love of binding – as the most analytical craftsman the trade has produced, Harrison provided the answers to several technical stumbling blocks. Such is the respect in which Harrison is held that a privately sponsored trade competition for novice and inexperienced bookbinders was named after him. This competition was later taken over by Designer Bookbinders.

Another ingenious binder, although understandably better known for his craftsmanship than his inventions, is Sydney Cockerell, who with his wife still runs the bindery founded by his father, Douglas. Born in 1906, Sydney (generally known as Sandy) was fortunate enough to become one of Douglas' pupils at the Central School. When he was eighteen he joined his father in the new bindery set up at their home in Letchworth, and embarked on a career remarkably similar to that of his senior partner. Having deputised for him at Central School he actually took over the post when Douglas retired in 1935. He did the same in 1938 at the Royal College of Art, and in 1945 at University College.

Over the years Sydney Cockerell has become identified more with conservation, and much of his fine binding has the distinctive quality of the designer Joan Rix Tebbutt. But it would be wrong to see him as merely the son of an outstanding father. He has made his own mark in several areas, principally in the materials and tools he uses. He is widely known for pioneering work (with his brother Oliver) in the production of marbled paper for doublures and endpapers. Although today the paper is sometimes

Daphnis and Chloe, designed and executed by Sydney Cockerell and Joan Rix Tebbutt in toned vellum with gold and black tooling.

regarded as abstract art and sheets of it are framed; in the 1920s, when they began, this was considered a debased craft. The brothers experimented with the marbling process which consists (basically) of floating colours on a thin solution made from the seaweed carrageen, the colours being drawn into patterns which are transferred to paper. The breakthrough came when the patterns could be controlled and made to order. Much of the success is due to William Chapman, who joined the bindery in 1931, and became probably the most skilled marbler. The Cockerell bindery also became known for its work in vellum, and Sydney has designed tools and equipment for that purpose, such as an adjustable mounted fillet for tooling parallel lines on vellum, and – even more ingenious – the adaptation of an aeroplane's flap ram into a pneumatic press designed to work gold and colour on to vellum. Another of his designs was for a binder's electric finishing stove, of which some 500 have been made.

Sydney Cockerell took over the firm on the death of his father in 1945, and eighteen years later moved to a site near Cambridge. Whether to maintain his own very high standards, or whether because of his reputation, he has always attracted assistants of quality, among them modern designer-binders, such as Philip Smith and James Brockman.

Roger Powell, former partner in the Cockerell bindery and a lifelong friend of Sydney, was born in 1896, which makes him the oldest craft binder still active, and enables him to span the years between traditional and 'modern' cover design. Although a disciple of Douglas Cockerell and part of the modern movement, he does not like much of what has happened in recent years, and much of his work today is on repair and conservation. Meeting a man approaching ninety who behaves like someone half his age (and drives a car with the verve of a teenager), and is still kept awake at night wrestling with a particular conservation problem, is an enlightening experience, reminding one that a craftsman never stops learning. On the day I last called at the bindery near Petersfield, he was working on a Hebrew Haggadah, dated 1527 – not especially old, but exceptionally rare, recently purchased at auction for $143,000 by the Valmadonna Trust of Zurich.

Considering his background – bookbinding goes back to his great-grandfather, to whom it was a hobby,

51

through to his uncle Edgar, a good amateur, having taken lessons from Douglas Cockerell, and his father, a master at Bedales School who included bookbinding among his subjects – Powell came to it relatively late in life. Having gone straight from school into the services in World War I, Roger joined his brother in a poultry farming operation until 1930, and then applied to join the Central School of Arts & Crafts. It was Douglas Cockerell who used his influence to get him a place after the Principal had virtually decided to reject him as too old. Among his teachers was William Matthews.

Many binders have characteristic styles, or fairly regular features in their work, and lettering – both conventional and 'distorted' – is something which has appeared frequently in Powell's designs. This he attributes half-jokingly to his shock at the cost of tools when he started; on the spot he decided to stick to the cheapest, which are letters of the alphabet, gouges, pallets and dots. Whatever the reason, he has always used them to good effect, even on the board edges.

In 1935 he joined the Cockerell bindery, becoming a partner in the following year. During World War II he went back to Central School to teach at a time when most of the lessons were conducted in a basement because of the air-raids – the building being hit on one occasion. In the last couple of years of Cockerell's life, when he was too ill to continue teaching, Powell also took over from him at the Royal College of Art, which had been evacuated to the country. Powell stayed at the Royal College of Art until 1956 when he was succeeded by one of his own pupils, Peter Waters.

Powell parted company with Sydney Cockerell in 1947 and set up his own bindery at Froxfield, Hampshire. His first prestige commission was from Trinity College, Dublin, to rebind the historic *Book of Kells* – the first of many similar assignments, including a sixth-century psalter – and because this meant spending three months in Dublin, Peter Waters was brought in to run the bindery; he stayed, with other commitments, until he became a partner in 1956. Waters eventually left to take up a post as Conservator at the Library of Congress in Washington.

While I do not accept Powell's prejudice towards many of the younger binders, it would be wrong to dismiss his views as being merely old-fashioned. For an enthusiast for 'modern' binding it is too easy to fall into the trap of writing off traditional work, on principle. Professional binders with an appreciation of fine craftsmanship object merely to 'copying', realising that what a sixteenth- or seventeenth-century binder did was at the time as modern as the efforts of his counterparts today. Some of Powell's creative bindings are very interesting, if unspectacular, and to his consternation they have risen dramatically in value. As he says: 'Like nearly all of the showpieces for which I have been asked the blame is mine entirely, from the sewing to the varnishing. It has a sobering effect on a designer. I am more interested in the book as a whole and its behaviour after I'm gone, than in doing something different on the outside.'

4
ATTITUDES TO MODERN BINDING

Someone once said that philosophy is about 'unintelligible answers to insoluble problems'. In creative binding there are no insoluble problems; not even problems in that sense – merely differences in interpretation of the 'rules'. Scratch the surface, and the divisions among professional binders are clearly defined. Having gained a reasonably clear understanding of what is generally meant by 'fine' binding, and the path it has followed in this century, you may wonder why, in the 1980s, there are still fundamental disagreements and misunderstandings.

The more one examines this question, the more complex it becomes. Are there two (or even three) separate movements, or just one and the same fragmented body? Are we talking about the *craft* of bookbinding, or the *art*? Have modern binders departed too far from the original concept of protecting a book in a pleasing manner? There are no cut-and-dried answers; more a qualified 'Yes', 'No', 'Perhaps' or 'Depends . . .'

The views of the many talented people involved in binding today cannot be lumped together with a couple of broad labels for the sake of convenience. The differences go beyond the original distinction between 'trade' and 'private', but even then it is not a case of instantly recognisable factions taking opposing stands, depending on whether they have an arts or crafts background. Indeed, binder A may agree with binder B in opposing the views of binder C, yet may well take C's side on issues in which he or she disagrees with B. There are many different philosophies, and little common ground on which they can be fairly evaluated. The reason, perhaps, is that in such a tight-knit little world, it is difficult to step back to obtain a wider perspective of the arguments.

The main rift has its origins at the beginning of the century, but although the gap between the two groups became wider the situation was more easily clarified in 1955 when Bernard Middleton and Arthur Johnson, representing the 'modern' movement, formed the Guild of Contemporary Bookbinders, with Edgar Mansfield as its first president. In 1968 the Guild was replaced by Designer Bookbinders. It retained the same objectives of promoting and exhibiting the art of the hand-bound book through modern binding, but by establishing a constitution, aimed at attracting a supporting body of friends and associates, to reach a wider audience and thus to stimulate growth in the activity and help advance its *recognition as an art*. Almost immediately, apprehension was expressed by a few respected figures that, in consciously moving towards art, they were losing sight of their roots – in binding. Roger Powell, who had been awarded an Honorary Fellowship of the Designer Bookbinders, was one who subsequently resigned. But the 'new' movement continued to gain momentum, although even today some of its most progressive Fellows are quick to point out that while hand binding is an art-form, they stop short of regarding it as a fine Art (the capital letter being reserved for a few disciplines such as painting).

The way binders interpret these guidelines is a major issue, and it would be useful to establish some common ground from which to try to understand the positions adopted by some of those involved. We can start by trying to define the meaning of two such emotive words as 'art' and 'craft'. The dictionary is not helpful, art being described in one as 'skill applied to imitation and design', and craft as 'a branch of skilled handicraft'. There are a dozen-and-one permutations of the above, suitably expanded, but few would argue with Art being the use of creative imagination to transform concepts, ideas and feelings into a 'physical' form which communicates them, through the senses, to the receiver. The varying degrees of success of whatever the physical form is, depends on the quality of the concept it manifests, and that being communicated by its presence.

It is, of course, one thing to define a word in isolation; something else to agree on that same word in

One of Bernard Middleton's bindings (1983). For *The Development & Usage of Brass Plate Dies* by Samuel Ellenport, he featured a sixteenth-century illustration from the book – by making a block and using it *reversed* in a recessed panel so that the background is pressed down. The binding is in black and yellow goatskin, the panel in dark green; the tooling was done freehand.

54

the context of different environments, which is why such men as Picasso have been so controversial in their time. Craft is a less sensitive word; it is best defined as a process using skills to make something out of unformed materials by way of a plan or design, although 'design' in this context can also represent a concept or feeling developed by the imagination. Philip Smith is explicit on the issue:

The artist working with the book can transform it physically to produce new insights and new feelings which, taken together with the content of the book, will give *more*. Art is a product of higher consciousness; craft is the product of physical skills. The third factor or intermediary is 'designing', which acts to produce an ordered representation of the tenuous or volatile insight for 'fixing' in a tangible form accessible to the senses of both the artist and others. Designing is an intellectual process; it is worked out on certain rules of composition. Decoration, which has been the traditional surface application, is not a product of higher consciousness, but one of contrivance, mental and physical manipulation, and craft skill. An *artist* can transform a surface or structure beyond decoration, and 'applied art'.

'New insights . . . taken together with the content of the book . . .': Smith was echoing one of the fundamental assertions of Designer Bookbinders, that it is dishonest for a creative person simply to copy an eighteenth-century binding in the style of the original; that book and binding have to be integrated, and that one of the priorities is to capture the essence of the message the author is trying to convey, and then interpret it in visual form – which does not have to be illustrative. The decoration – as apparent from the illustrations in this book – can take any form, so long as the binder is following the same basic criteria.

When one sees an old binding with its elaborate tooling and almost standard decoration, it is obvious that traditionally the book's content was not much considered by binders. Yet it is not the link between content and cover to which the traditionalists object, but the way in which the function of the binding has changed. Roger Powell resigned because he considered the pace-setters were going too far when their designs – incorporating attachments and extensions and featuring lines that 'interfere' with shape and form – no longer looked like what we have been conditioned to accept as a book. That is, of course, a sweeping statement, but the point is worthy of amplification. 'We mustn't deny the form and mechanics of a book in the way that it handles in order to satisfy your ideas.

Many are bas-relief and fine as hangings, but not as the cover of a book to be opened,' he maintains. It remains, however, a minority view among individual binders today.

So if the purists do not contest the principle of the binding being an extension of the author's message, who does? One, surprisingly, is Ivor Robinson – among the world's most highly regarded binders, a leading figure in the Designer Bookbinders and its President from 1968 to 1973. When he began, Robinson had not formulated a considered viewpoint and was quite happy to respond to the emotive qualities of a literary work. But for several years, flying in the face of the beliefs of his friends and colleagues, he has insisted that the binding should stand as a work of visual creativity in its own right, alongside the contribution of several people whose craftsmanship is featured in the book's production; he maintains that to ask a binder, untrained in anything except his speciality, to interpret the work of an author, especially of the more obscure texts, is 'bloody naive'.

Obviously Robinson cannot and does not object to a binding carrying a message, if that is the binder's decision, but as a starting-off point he insists the philosophy is wrong:

Your medium is a three-dimensional object, and if you're going to bind a 3-D object, the first relationship you have to make is to reconcile what you are doing with 3 D – in other words, with the book as an *object*, not the book as a carrier of text. The next relationship is towards the materials you intend to use, in preserving, protecting, completing this 3-D object. This done, you have to find a method of working appropriate to you as a visual artist . . . that is an extension of your fingers – in a sense, an extension of your brain . . . something that comes naturally to you as an expressive medium for anything you want to express.

If you are creative in the sense that you have a compulsion to make something, to activate a surface . . . this can come out in a number of ways, in writing, in making a print . . . but if it happens to come out in binding a book, then the artefact you're making must allow this expression of whatever you've got inside. It so happens that some books – not all books – carry an author's text. There are books to be read, to be looked at, always to be partly read and partly looked at. The book to be read is only one of a number of different ways in which the book is apprehended and used. In the production of books are the crafts of all sorts of people – the paper maker (possibly someone who makes parchment or vellum), the calligrapher perhaps, the typographer, graphic designer, photographer or illustrator . . . and the author. I don't think your job as a binder is to relate to any of these to the exclusion of the others; you've got to apprehend the book as a total entity.

The problem is that if you face a blank piece of canvas, you can make a mark on that canvas without actually having to weave that canvas or stretch it. But with a book you've actually got to bind it *before* you can start putting those marks on. At some point this artefact has to carry what you want to say, in the same way as a piece of canvas, or a piece of wood if you're carving it. I think to put the binder in an interpretative position denies the independence of the binder as a creative person in his own right – which is not to say that you ignore the contents of a book; but the prime responsibility is to the form and the materials.

Robinson becomes even more controversial when he talks of his own method of working. Conceding that one need not ignore the contents of a book, he insists that he would be able to justify his designs in relation to the text 'if put to it'; but taking his theme to its logical conclusion, surely such designs might almost be done in advance of the book? His answer is that they are! Then how would he tackle three such diverse books as (say) Melville's *Moby Dick*, James Joyce's *Ulysses*, and perhaps the centenary report of a trade or professional body? Would he not approach them very differently?

'I like to *keep* drawing designs for bookbinding,' he says, using Henry Moore as an analogy because of the way Moore constantly draws designs for his sculpture:

My motivation is the book as a three-dimensional object, and it is the way my lines activate the surface to find that extra dimension. If I can find a book that fits an existing design, I'm much happier. Very often that sort of relationship of drawing and book is for me far better than if I sit down with a book in front of me and try to cook up a design for it, because I think that creates a self-conscious activity which destroys spontaneity.

To the best of my knowledge, Ivor Robinson is the only important binder who works in this way. To colleagues who disagree with his views, he says: 'To say that the binding must relate to the text is so naive. What do you do with Dante? What presumption has someone who has never done any art training, or visual training – and this applies to 60 per cent of the people working in the orbit of the Designer Bookbinders – got to say '*I* can interpret Dante'?

Another book artist who takes a similar stand to Robinson, yet has more in common with those who regard the binding as an art object – to the extent that many of his works carry no text at all – is Bruce Schnabel of Los Angeles. He believes that the traditional function of the book as communicator has obscured our appreciation of other aspects of the book form:

Because the book has come to perform as a neutral vehicle of information, the primacy of reading has eclipsed the 'object' quality. Recent developments in methods of communications, information storage and retrieval, word processing and computers make us question the efficiency of books in their modern historic role. New technologies have in many ways relieved the book of its manifest function, giving freedom to revitalise its form and broaden its scope. The book is a medium for artists to explore.

Admittedly, Philip Smith was saying much the same thing several years ago, but Bruce Schnabel's interpretation of 'revitalising' its form is different, and his career has been motivated by different goals. Like the painters who have successfully defied convention, he is an excellent craftsman, and his work reflects this duality of talent. To use his own words, 'making books is both a discipline and a creative release.' It also means that his books (in general) are no longer functional as transmitters of literary ideas, because he concentrates on the sculptural and textural qualities. Even when Schnabel does use the codex/conventional form (and he has had a thorough training in binding, restoration and conservation, so that he respects the traditional form), it is his intention that the cover should be as interesting as the content. The breakaway does not mean that Schnabel has become disenchanted with the literary vehicle; on the contrary, he still accepts commissions for an 'appropriate' design binding in the conventional idiom (as indeed he does for period bindings). In fact it was a revolt against the 'abstract-expressionistic' interpretations of literature that many modern binders produce that prompted him to explore his own 'aesthetic sensibilities'.

Because of his regard for 'technical' excellence, Schnabel is not afraid to call on the specialist talents of other artists, and some of his works are fascinating collaborations, which themselves introduce an extra dimension. While partnerships between designers and binders are not uncommon (indeed, are the norm in France), Schnabel's concept of total collaboration from the outset is extremely unusual. In 1983 the results were still being created speculatively for exhibitions, and then sold; once the concept is properly understood and the participating artists known and accepted,

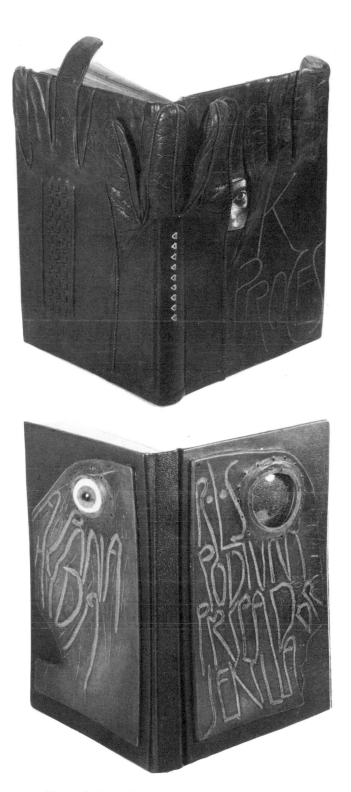

Few of Jiri Hadlač's bindings are similar, but both these two feature a human eye in different guises. For Kafka's *Der Prozess* (1981) a face peers from between the fingers of a black glove (the glove on the rear board is brown). In the same year he bound this edition of Robert Louis Stevenson's *Dr Jekyll and Mr Hyde* with a glass eye set into the leather on the back cover, counterbalanced with a piece of optical glass on the front.

commissions will come. Bruce Schnabel explains his philosophy of collaboration as follows:

I believe that collaborations allow people to multiply their creative energies geometrically. Each artist (myself and others) can work as an individual and simultaneously each loses their ego to a single project; can rely on intuition as well as personal technical vocabulary, and share a common creative vision. The finished work is something that neither or none of the collaborators could have imagined on their own. All design ideas are shared from concept; the technical aspects of the project are worked out by whoever has the

most information, in conjunction with fresh ideas and inspirations which may come from the other. This cross fertilisation allows each participating collaborator to be artist/designer/binder.

Some traditionalists will dismiss Schnabel as a 'gimmick merchant', muttering about people who haven't yet learnt how to bind; but they will have to discover that other, more 'experienced', binders are beginning to investigate the no-text avenue – such men as Jiri Hadlač from Brno in Czechoslovakia, the country with a tradition in binding as distinguished as its better-known association with glass. Hadlač and his countrymen Jan Vrtílek and Jan Sobota (now living in Switzerland) are among the world's top binders, and each has a forward-looking approach.

All are innovators, but Hadlač, also a talented

For Kafka's *Metamorphose*, Jiri Hadlač has used white leather; it is set on a metal stand, the only design, apart from the tooled lettering, being ball-bearings held behind glass.

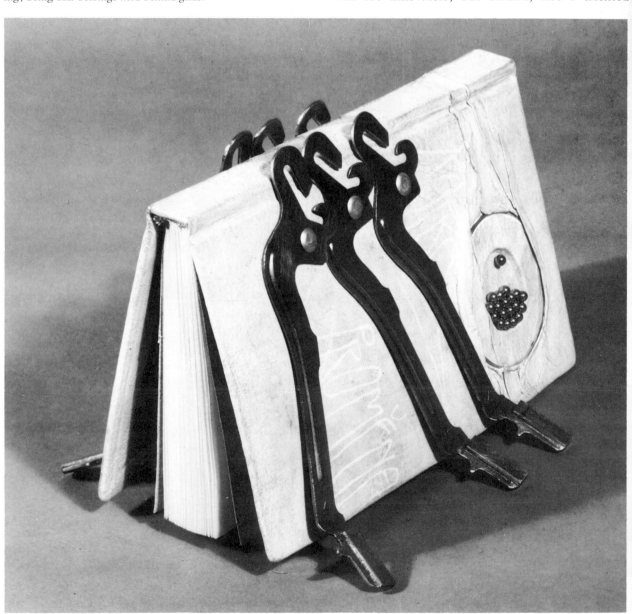

wood-sculptor, is another who does not need to gain his inspiration from an author – although obviously he can do so, and has done. He is beginning to experiment with bindings for books that have no text – but would be textless picture-books, rather than offering Schnabel's abstract patterns – or with books he has prepared himself, rather than having a separate author. Traditional print is already beginning to make way, and in one of his latest bindings, *In the Penal Colony*, a Kafka short story, the text is written in coloured ink on brown and sand-coloured paper. The format is very large (roughly 18 × 12in, 46 × 31cm) and slim, a shape on which Hadlač prefers to work. It is covered from pieces of an old leather jacket, complete with pocket and button-holes, and decorated with a relief made from a horse collar and a few small brass objects.

Meanwhile, to return to the question of interpretation, one of the answers may be found among the symbolic, as opposed to illustrative, designs shown in

While teaching at the New York Center for Book Arts, David Sellars bound this Nonesuch Press edition of *Miscellaneous Poems*, by Andrew Marvell. It is an illustration of his belief in capturing the spirit of a book, and that a binding should have a tactile quality, not be just something to look at from a distance. Marvell's poems are metaphysical, posing questions of life and death, but never answered; Sellars has created a binding which is a representation of a twentieth-century parallel to the metaphysical approach of the seventeenth century. The series of cheap snap fasteners – male on the front; female on the back – would snap together to provide the answers to questions raised in the poems – but can't get to each other because of the spine barrier. Throwaway products (the fasteners) are elevated to high art, and in turn represent the trappings used to protect the book in early bindings.

The book itself is bound in a linen canvas and then onlaid with tiny fragments of leather, into which the studs are inlaid. To create a sculptural effect it has been coated with a varnish mixture of leather dust and polyvinyl acetate adhesive. The doublures are in a contrastingly soft texture – goatskin split down the centre to highlight the different dyed hues. So that the book can also be shown as a piece of sculpture, it is set in a wooden frame covered in fragments of leather.

this book. An interesting example is Andrew Marvell's *Miscellaneous Poems*, bound by David Sellars, whose views are basically opposed to those of Ivor Robinson, yet who considers him to have made one of the major contributions to fine binding in the past two decades. Indeed, intense though he is, Sellers is more receptive than most in his flexibility towards rules, acknowledging the right of others to find their own motivation.

To most professional craftsmen or artists, any commission must be welcome, but Sellars, another binder with an arts background, happens to regard the author's message as sacrosanct. When in 1612 Francis Bacon wrote 'Some books are to be tasted, others to be swallowed, and a few to be chewed and digested' (*Essays: Of Studies*), he might have been anticipating Sellars' binding philosophy. If after 'chewing and digesting' for months, or even years, he is still not satisfied that he can interpret the author's flavour, he will decline a commission as he explains:

Many binders don't engage in a philosophical discourse with the medium. I question the medium every day. It's not good enough just because you're doing an apparently straight-forward book about bees to knock out a design incorporating a bee. Unless you are prepared to go all the way, the work is no good. I can have a book two or three years; when the time is right it comes – but it may never come. I have to read the book several times until I have identified with it utterly. It has to be about me, got to become *my* book, or the work is a disservice to the author. *Finnegan's Wake* became part of my thinking, and that way I could express it in book form.

I admire the work of David Sellars – and he enjoys establishing a creative partnership with James Joyce. It is not in criticism that I ask if such agonising is necessary, but because of a point raised in a letter to me from Edgar Mansfield, whose work demonstrated that, in his case, the relationship between binder and author was usually in his treatment of the *material* used, his design being in the main abstract. 'Decoration is the celebration, and personal signature of the binder,' he wrote, using 'celebration' as in the festive dance of joy. 'What matters really is *not* so much the philosophy of the designer, however forcefully or repeatedly stated, but the quality of the design itself, and it is here that weaknesses show. Creation is sometimes confused with novelty, and it is here that integration and technical skill are sometimes ignored, so that the result merely intimidates the observer.'

The theme is developed by Philip Smith, a constant pace-setter, as his writing on the subject reveals. In his

The Book: Art & Object, he maintains: 'Design is so often left to the end as something cosmetic instead of being used as the organising principle of the whole. Good designing, good drawing and sound bookbinding methods are essential partners in the liberation of imagination through this medium. And don't forget, the freedom to *create* is not gained without the hard discipline of learning to *make* well.' And even critics, such as his former tutor, concede that Philip Smith's craftsmanship cannot be faulted. Answering them, Philip Smith says:

We are not producing books for shelves; there is no need to do that by hand with the mass production book-culture. Something else needed to be developed, giving a more multi-dimensional quality and look to the book form. The purist/functionalist bookbinders, ie in the traditional sense, see no need for anything more if you are merely preserving literature between strongly attached flat boards – but there is the human spirit, the joy of making, the search for wholeness – in fact, the creative urge, to be taken into consideration in the sheer love of making. So the new theme is going beyond merely preserving literature.

The literature itself is the inspiration for new modes of expression; beyond illustration, beyond decoration; it is a search beyond mere application of contemporary art styles to flat surfaces, but an aspect of bringing attention to the three- (and indeed, four-dimensional) nature of the book by standing it as an object transformed by human creativity with its own individuality, and meaningfulness.

What I am searching for is a way of delineating that particular book with a new expression of its individuality – for an expression without words of the *personality* of that particular book. So in the declining years of the need to bind books by hand for reading, a quite new approach is being developed. It should be made clear that the handful of true pioneers are not competing with the 'craft-binders' because the traditionalists cannot or will not see that our aims are in a totally different world.

We are not competing with them . . . more, trying to provide new material to *add* to a cultural heritage that we too are anxious to preserve. The more the things seem different, the more it is the same, but with an added evolutionary thrust. Followers and students often imitate the gesture without realising the motivation of the originator, until they can begin to see their own contribution from their own experience and individuality. Then they take off on one or other facet, an idea, a technique or whatever, and eventually develop something that is their own.

The six-unit book wall for Tolkien's *Lord of the Rings*, a book which
has inspired Philip Smith on a number of occasions.

Discussing the inevitability of the link between binding and text, Smith refers to the new ground broken by the 'evocative' bindings of Legrain and Bonet, which appeared in the main to be geometric abstractions:

The French (and others) feared the 'illustrative' or the figurative style as being either sentimental or banal, overlooking the fact that illustration is mainly associated with books and literature and therefore a logical choice if book and binding are to relate visually. Nevertheless the didactic statements about 'relationship to text' jammed a wedge in the door and before long it became an accepted tenet of the art; the door was soon opened to a flood of interpretations of this concept.

Smith shares Ivor Robinson's attitude to the book as an art object in its own right (although obviously disagreeing over the relation between binder and author), and in 1968 introduced the concept of 'book walls', which have never been developed but provide an answer to those who protest that by reducing a book to an object is to deny its main feature – its readability. The 'book walls' were originally started as a centrepiece for a one-man show, with designs that were complete in themselves, yet when set out in tiled pattern created a landscape effect. It took Smith two years to design and produce Tolkien's *Lord of the Rings* in twenty-one 'pictures' (symbolically seven sets of three volumes). As an exhibit it was instantly acclaimed, but no one had conceived such an art form, so there was no rush to buy. He was on the point of selling the seven sets individually, when it was purchased by the bookdealer and collector Colin Franklin.

A leading American bookseller, Bernard Breslauer, attacked the concept as 'a travesty against the book', making books inaccessible as literature. Smith and his supporters deny this, claiming that the books are no more inaccessible than certain books in many distinguished libraries; indeed, with the perspex cover removed the books can be read – ideally, aloud – by up to seven people, each with a different binding.

Returning to the theme of change, he writes in *The Book: Art & Object*:

It was necessary to move away from the 'embellished' book to the 'book as an art object' before a new outlook could become possible and established, with the work considered just as highly but from a quite different standpoint of psychological and aesthetic interpretation. The history of art does not show sudden breaks with tradition. There are always precedents leading up

to a new style or a new outlook, with transitional stages. Break-throughs often depend on the bringing together of several diverse or isolated elements into a new whole, and have to bide their time until the ingredients required are available. Such was Gutenberg's amalgamation of the principles of the coin punch, the seal and the wine press to invent printing from moveable types.

So Ivor Robinson describes the bound book as an object, while Philip Smith refers to the *art* object. Needless to add, further opinions are just as divided; even more so when it comes to agreeing on a definition of progress.

Faith Shannon, one of the most versatile and talented English binders, whose background is also in art (she teaches, as well as supplementing her income with illustrations of a very high standard for books and advertising), regards bookbinding as no more important than any other of the art disciplines: 'Some of my colleagues are worried that we've been left behind, but I don't see it as a race. It is a fact, though, that in terms of public appeal, *graphics* is the fastest developing arts category, and one has only to look at the Crafts Council's collection of slides to see what an influence graphics has had on other arts.' She is, of course, thinking predominantly of advertising, in which graphics and bright colours spearhead the appeal to the individual's magpie inclinations, the subconscious desire to acquire possessions.

Ivor Robinson, choosing to talk of 'visual activity' rather than 'fine art', takes up the question of status:

So much has happened in the art world that you can take slices of bread, tie a rope round them, and exhibit the result as a visual activity and call it 'buying bread'. It's for reasons like this I don't see much point in wasting time trying to break down barriers in craft, and trying to push craft into fine art – when people who had art training are saying that Art isn't necessarily about status in material . . . it's about how you *apply* your material, how you *frame* the material, about what gallery you put them into . . . it's about taking objects

Trevor Jones finds humour in most situations, and especially in James Joyce, often taken so seriously. In this 1959 binding of *Finnegan's Wake* he features the swirling chaos of Creation, with 'big Mr Finnegan' falling off his ladder on the front cover. Jones glued a scattering of caraway seeds and lentils on the boards, and some strips of lino cuttings, to make relief shapes and textures under the leather. When the time came to cover it with black oasis goatskin he decided to push it around and see what happened. This was the first time he had manipulated leather to enhance the grain, although he discovered later it had been a subconscious action, probably inspired by ideas derived from Edgar Mansfield.

as Picasso did when he took a bike saddle and the handlebars and said this was a bull. I don't think one has to worry about this. You produce a piece of work as well as you are able, until it says what you want it to say, and you exhibit it – and it is judged on that basis.

On the need for change or 'progress', he says: 'If you look around at the people who have made their mark in the visual arts then the great ones weren't always moving forward. Look at Henry Moore, and you can see a natural development. Look at Ben Nicholson and Victor Passmore and you can see a natural logical development; they weren't always skidding off and doing something else. Even with Picasso you can still see a natural development.'

As always there is another side. Trevor Jones of York, another of the most accomplished binders, and President of the Designer Bookbinders in 1983, does not disagree but sees it differently. 'Playing safe is no formula for success in art. The need to take risks is surely important – to be setting out on an adventure with each new binding. Perhaps what I'm most against in binding is the idea of the "precious object", which is why I've been heard to talk of designing bad tastes into bindings.' Jones is a binder who tries to find the 'humour' in a book on which he is working – being prepared to turn down a commission if he feels no sympathy for the book as a book – and is far less reverent than many of his contemporaries. One of the techniques that sums up his philosophy is his use of scraps of leather taken from unlikely places, parts of an old handbag or glove, even flotsam from a beach. Their application is usually stimulating, as my illustrations show.

Having commented earlier on French attitudes to design, one has to say that the overwhelming success of Paul Bonet and some of his disciples introduced a degree of complacency in that country for a number of years. Fine binding continued to be produced, but there was far less challenge to what was accepted as the ideal than from contemporaries across the English Channel. However, that was to change with the arrival on the scene of two outstanding binders, Daniel Knoderer and Jean de Gonet, whose work is discussed more fully later. It was these men who questioned what was happening, were not satisfied with the answers, and came up with their own, different solutions.

Although respectful of Legrain particularly, the Parisian de Gonet (one of the very few French binders who began by executing his own work) has reacted against the vivid decoration used by so many other French designers – usually more like thoughtless imitations of the work of artists featured inside the

(right) Bruce Schnabel produced *Silk Screens*, a concertina book of designs, in 1982. The binding is of Nigerian goatskin, with goat and calf onlay, screen impressions, silk stitching and glass seed beads. The hand-dyed silk is stitched to a fibreglass screen; silk threads and beads are inset in covered mats with hand-dyed silk borders and hinges.

(below right) Tim Ely generally conceives a book as a whole and then 'edits' that form so that it is technically feasible for him to represent it. Sometimes a page is graphically dynamic enough to be developed as the cover structure, but more often the theme comes intuitively. For *Silences and Distances* (1983) the boards are covered with handmade Japanese paper, tooled in black and silver and blind. Large areas of drawing are onlaid, along with leather over black French mould-made paper; the circles are deep-recessed on-lays. Oasis goatskin is used for the spine, forming the tongue that enters the slotted board.

(overleaf) Faith Shannon had contemplated binding Lewis Carroll's *Alice Through the Looking Glass* since her Royal College days. For this commission from the Crafts Council in 1973, she re-read the text and was struck by a passage describing the mirror turning into a silvery mist; she chose silver kid, inlaid on dark-red oasis. Alice was formed in bleached linen, painted and quilted into shape with embroidery stitches, each section stuffed with kapok. The completed 'doll' was countersunk into the leather.

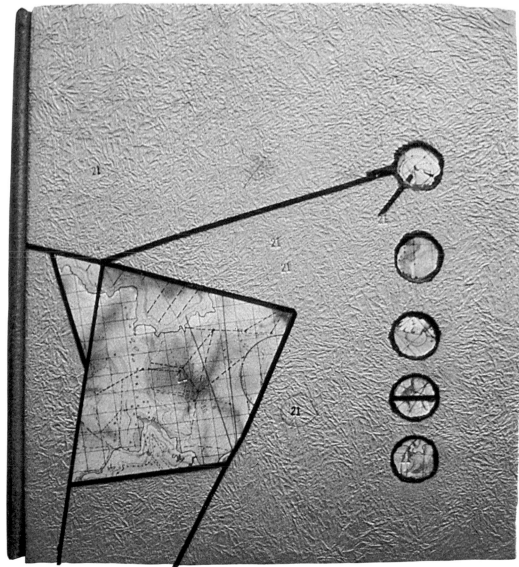

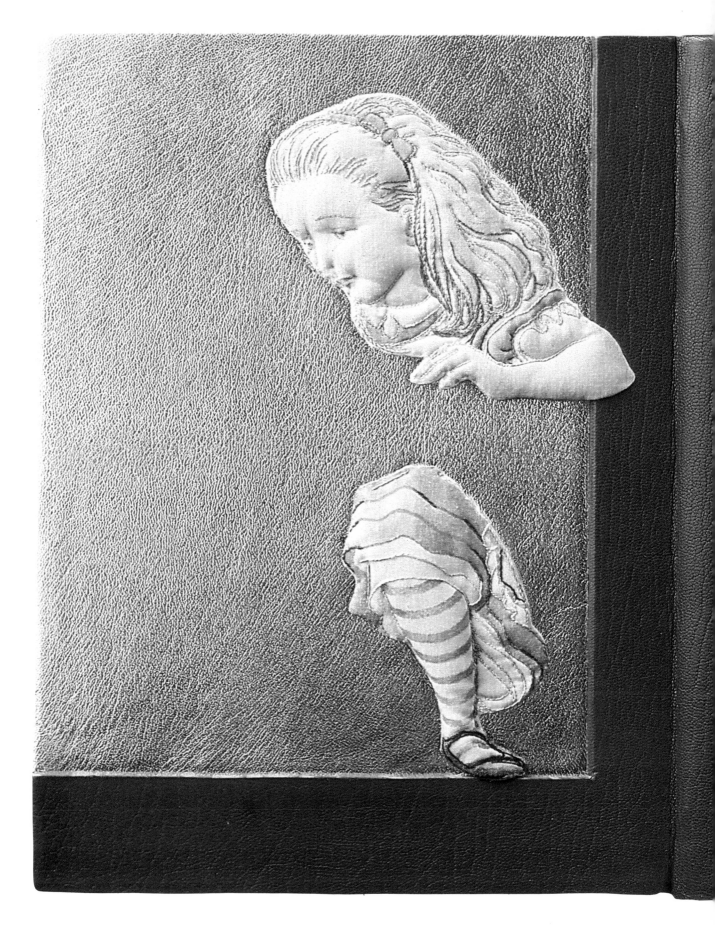

book than truly creative expression. Regarding the book as an artefact and finding no need to represent the author, de Gonet's bindings are inspired by the *structure*, the assembly through sewing, which to him is more important than all other considerations. The fact that there is a clinical beauty about his ostensibly plain but very distinctive work, is almost incidental, because de Gonet is seeking a sense of participation; it is best experienced when actually holding one of his bindings, to appreciate its tactile qualities. He explains:

The 'talking' binding, where the decorator was directly inspired by the text or the illustrations, did not exclude some considerable successes, but more often than not it distanced the bookbinder from the real basis of his craft, and thereby from the authentic creation. My principal goal has been to lighten bookbinding of its descriptive message, and to envisage it solely in its powerful materiality. The effort of research goes essentially into the materials, the multiple working techniques, and their interaction.

Daniel Knoderer, of Valbonne, France, whose parents were binders, and who was playing at the craft at an age when most children's fantasies revolve around fairytales and toys, was not long in becoming aware of the traditional restrictions imposed on binders, both in form and materials. As a result, he began to experiment in sculptural forms, using the usual materials decorated with others less conventional, such as metal, wood, polyester, glass, paint and miscellaneous objects. He found this gave him greater freedom of expression, while retaining the legibility and function of the book:

If the bookbinder feels completely free, he will offer the art lover original works whose functions are diverse and whose effects are unprecedented. This will enable him to play a game with the bookbinder – the game of surprise, imagination and perception. This actually happens with some of my customers who may receive new creations with conflicting emotions . . . of

surprise, even shock – but who are won over by an idea or conception which is new to them. This exchange between artist and customer is very important.

The same need to communicate provided the motivation for Timothy C. Ely, of New York, an outstanding 'total book' artist. First and foremost, Ely is an artist who wanted his drawings and paintings viewed as a series – not hung on a wall or peered at through glass. His notebooks provided the answer – books. To him the book is a 'looking-at' machine. The problem with many total-book enthusiasts is that though they tackle one operation well, they may remain amateurish in disciplines outside their immediate interest. Ely set out to research and learn both binding and papermaking, so that his striking work does not consist of talented drawings and paintings with a cover crudely stuck on, but can be an integrated whole. Typically, he is less critical of some of his contemporaries. 'I do not want my books damaged by accident or through process suicide. This does not mean I discount paper between clay tablets tied with linen as frivolous – only dangerously fragile.'

Finally, to return to basics, let us hear from someone whose binding is part of his philosophy of life. Lage Eric Carlson, born in Sweden but brought up in the USA, says:

I am part of the American stream-line-so-called-happy-faster-better-living, but not attached to it. Part of my five years' training as a Zen monk and two years in India have influenced me to move in my own philosophical direction. A large part of this direction is my commitment to being a professional bookbinder. Bookbinding is a very small area in the way the world works but it allows me a tremendous freedom – freedom of expression in my work, great flexibility in my life style, and integrity in what I do. I feel very fortunate to be able to work without distraction, complete nearly all the processes myself and exercise the muscle of complete commitment.

The Genus Crocus (1886) represents the life's work of George Maw, and Faith Shannon's binding (1973) symbolises the depth of this botanical study. The spectacular image represents all that was seen through one man's eye (the crocus being related to the iris). The front board is modelled over the convex moulded shape of balsa wood and papier-mâché, in which is inlaid the 'eye' of painted vellum. In keeping with the timeless character of the book, she has borrowed the medieval idea of the cabuchon to protect delicate work on a binding – protecting the 'eye' with a specially blown shatterproof glass 'lid'. Marbled doublures and endpapers reflect the mood of the period when the book was written.

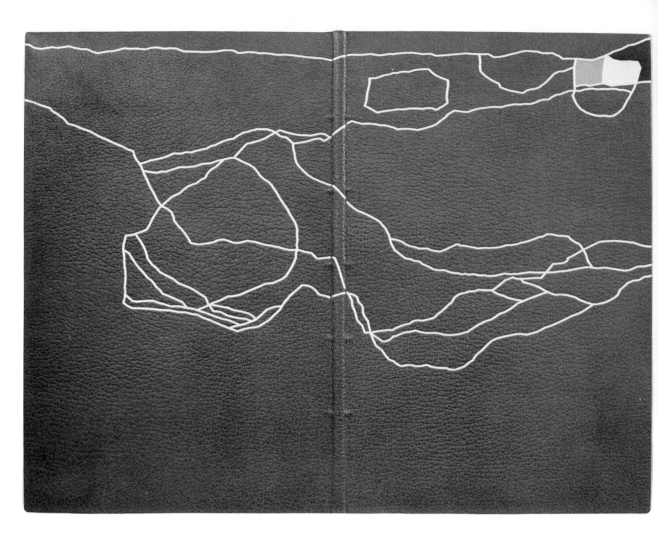

Two bindings by Ivor Robinson. *(above) On The Nativity of Christ*, 1974, uses brown goatskin with black, white and beige onlays. *The Lamentations of Jeremiah (below)*, 1982, is black goatskin with black and white calf onlays.

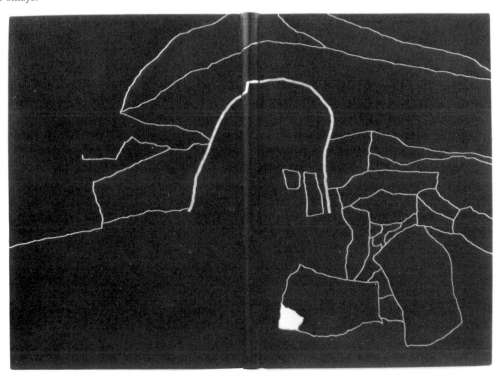

5

INNOVATION

In the sciences, one talks instinctively of progress; in the arts only of change – or perhaps an extension of scope – because the line of development in this context is horizontal and not vertical. Binding, just as other arts or crafts, has evolved in fits and starts, new ideas coming in the main as a logical extension of existing achievements. Most binders would agree that to sit down in front of a book to be bound and decide to 'be original' is unlikely to produce the desired results. True creativity comes (we tell ourselves) from an unconscious harnessing of trained resources – always assuming a degree of the necessary talent. Conversely, self-consciousness is likely to have an inhibiting effect.

The mould-breakers among writers and artists, the likes of Picasso or Joyce, probably do not consciously set out to establish new frontiers. Yet to all sweeping generalisations there must be exceptions. Where would we put Salvador Dali? Unquestionably he was an innovator, but consciously or unconsciously? It is possible that the answer lies in compromise; the artist craftsman setting out to experiment may be able to call upon an unquantifiable input from his subconscious.

Talent has little bearing on output, of course, but there has to be a difference in outlook between the binder who works full-time, or almost so, and who believes that innovation is a rejuvenating process, and the person who through choice or circumstance produces only infrequently over a given period. This is not to say that the more cautious elements must produce work that could be described as ordinary. Faith Shannon and Angela James, for example, both Fellows of the Designer Bookbinders, do not depend on creative binding for a living, and are dubious about innovation for its own sake; yet both are among the most interesting and versatile of modern binders.

The quality of Faith Shannon's work, and particularly her design, is such that her opinions matter. Her belief in the importance of subtlety and restraint is unquestionably a valid one. 'At times I have wanted to be exuberant in design, but had to squash that idea,

because that was not what the book was all about,' she says. She expresses the hope that her bindings differ widely enough (and they do, to most people) not to be recognised as her work. Yet most of her contemporaries claim they are able to recognise her touch. Says one: 'If it's not immediately identifiable as something by Faith, then at least we know it can't be by anyone else.'

She is also an advocate of simplicity. 'A binding can be so beautifully made that anyone realises it without necessarily understanding art,' she says. 'One is hardly aware of it, because of its simplicity. When there is a struggle of mind over matter, the activity can become self-conscious.' Incidentally, despite the strength of her own design, some of the binding she most admires is very plain, almost without decoration of any sort.

Angela James is also critical of innovation for its own sake. 'If it comes, that's fine,' she concedes. 'But not to force yourself.' Raising a similar issue, she adds: 'To produce something that is different is not necessarily producing something that is innovative. There appeared to be a problem in the jewellery field when people decided it was "old hat" to produce a plain gold ring. Now they have to design extraordinary wire-wear which is never going to be worn outside the exhibition gallery.' Yet neither she nor Faith Shannon are against change. She looks forward with excitement to the exhibitions of some of her colleagues' work to see what fresh ideas they will have come up with; whereas she concedes that others stand still, merely repeating 'the same old thing' in different colours.

Nevertheless, there have been a number of conscious efforts to extend the parameters of creativity, and some have established a pattern on which others could build. I have mentioned Edgar Mansfield's interest in the natural qualities of leather, in exploiting the grain in a number of ways, including 'puckering' or 'moulding' it, but whatever ingenuity is demonstrated leather does of course impose limitations. Binders do work in other materials, particularly textiles, but few of these have the versatility of leather; the options available with (say) satin or silk are also limited. These considerations went through the mind of James Brockman, another of the younger Fellows of the Designer Bookbinders (elected in 1972), when he read Philip Smith's *New Directions in Bookbinding* in 1975. Brockman's background is conventional. Having been apprenticed as a finisher at a trade bindery, and almost given up in boredom until his escape to Sydney Cockerell, he had established himself as a creative craftsman, but wanted to produce something that might more directly relate to the 'new directions' to which Smith was pointing. The result is a metal 'electronic' binding, as an alternative to leather, sewn in a conventional way, with the cover made of three brass frames with perspex each side. To illustrate Smith's theme, he asked Howard M. Nixon, then probably the leading authority on the history of binding, to list what he considered the most

James Brockman's first 'electronic' breakthrough, a binding for Philip Smith's *New Directions in Bookbinding*.

significant milestones in this experiment (in fact, there are sixteen such stages), suitably highlighted by lamp bulbs operated by switches – the power coming from rechargeable batteries in the spine and solar batteries. The back cover has miniature photographic colour reproductions of bindings suspended by black thread. A double-acting hinge allows the boards to open right back like an ordinary book.

What began as an experiment at Brockman's bindery in Oxford, was acclaimed by most impartial observers, and ended up in the Bridwell Library, in Dallas, Texas. Having made his point, Brockman returned to more conventional materials, although in 1979 he acceded to demand, and produced a more sophisticated electronic binding, *Beauty and Deformity*, described elsewhere.

The 'see-through' principle has been used in a different way by Bruce Schnabel, mentioned earlier in the context of no-text books and collaborations. Working with Harvey Redding, with whom he had

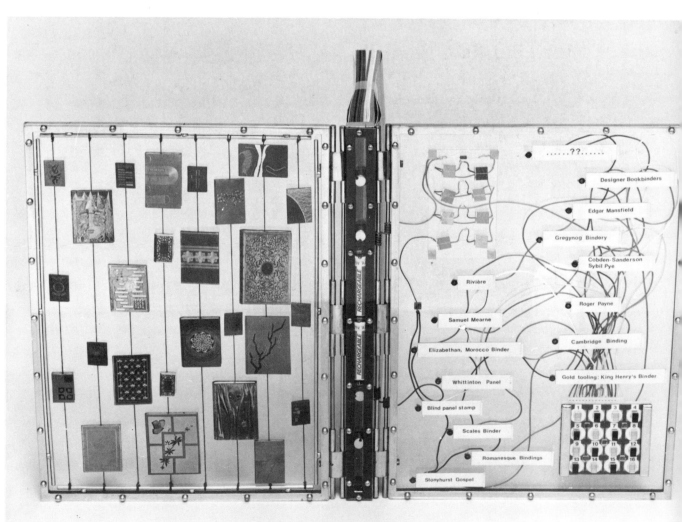

The Beaubourg Book (1980) by Bruce Schnabel and Harvey Redding.

collaborated in a number of book projects, some as early as 1971, he has produced the very interesting *Beaubourg Book* (1980). The two artists had been interested in the idea of creating a transparent book for a couple of years, but the inspiration came in Paris, from seeing the architecture of the Pompidou Centre, a celebration of structure as design. They decided to produce a book calling attention to its mechanics and workings as a work of art. Redding had been working with colour xerox and creating one-of-a-kind editions of postcards in that medium, and it was this that provided the logical 'text' – in fact it was a series of collaged photos from issues of *Popular Mechanics* magazine and tourist postcard images. Redding also designed the layouts, which they colour-xeroxed on acetate. The pages are plastic, as are the cords and threads. The boards are clear plexiglas with vinyl cover. The binding structure is traditional (or as Schnabel says, 'almost traditional'), with five raised cords.

It is the student who is likely to be more adventurous in the choice of materials, and the results are often effective. But one experiment that works brilliantly does not make a professional binder, and in the end most continue to work mainly in leather. So what can be done within the known limitations? When assessing the standards of professional binders, one looks for a positive statement in their work that is unique to them for a period. Many people believe that one of the most significant contributions of the past half-century was the decision of Ivor Robinson in the early 1970s to work only in sombre colours (predominantly black and/or brown), with the tooling in gold or white. It does not sound very significant, yet this 'statement', producing some remarkably striking bindings, was not a conscious decision to be innovative, but something which happened to suit Robinson's own philosophy of design and expression; it was not inspired by new dimensions but by the sixteenth century.

Trained as a binder, Robinson's early days were fairly conventional, but an enthusiasm for drawing drew him instinctively to tooling; it was largely the traditional floral-style decoration that he cut his teeth on. It was the work of John Mason (who wrote a textbook on binding, and taught at Leicester) which provided the eye-opening because his designs were mainly to do with horizontals, verticals and plain areas of colour. Robinson's designs began to feature straight lines, and later, looking at the work of French binders (and painters), he became fascinated by the concept of the subliminal jigsaw, in which a piece of a design fitted and related to others. He recalls:

At one point I was producing a grey binding featuring stripes – inlaying stripes in white so that they were level with the grey surface, and *on*laying black stripes over the white to get a black and white effect. I was interested in stripes but thought there must be a less tedious activity, so I reverted to tooling.

About the same time there was a wonderful exhibition of Jean Grolier bindings at the British Museum in 1965, and when I examined these fine sixteenth-century books, I suddenly wondered why we were playing around with colours and sticking bits of leather together. What bookbinding is all about is really leather and gold. The feeling was reinforced by a subsequent visit to an exhibition of English Restoration period bindings. I thought why are we trying to be painters, using coloured leather when the medium isn't the same. Painters can mix colours to get an infinite variety whereas we all buy leather from the same sources which means a certain uniformity is inevitable. Also, if I was going to work in gold, the best value I could get was to work it on black, or brown.

Indeed, Grolier and Robinson bindings could be described in the same terms: black or brown leather, tooled in gold, heightened (sometimes) with a little colour. The main difference between their approaches – apart from the design – is that Robinson limits his tools to about three. The other influence on this transformation was Robinson's skill in tooling, because, whatever his philosophical reasoning, no binder weak in that craft would have taken this course. Equally, because he gave up using colour he started designing with a pencil, and with a pencil one tends to use lines – which brings us back to tooling.

This conservation of effort was also, perhaps, a reaction against the trend towards expressive bindings with a mass of activity – onlays, inlays, cut-outs, sculptured additions or attachments. 'The more some people put into their bindings, the less I put in mine.' He uses painting to find analogies:

There is a story about Turner who went to a gallery and saw a Constable picture hanging alongside his own. It was the opening of Westminster Bridge with coloured flags and full of colour; Turner's was a grey seascape, grey sea, grey ship. Turner is supposed to have growled and put one little red blob in the sea before going away. When Constable came in he said, 'I see Turner's fired off a shot', but on varnishing day Turner came in and finished off the blob, turning it into a buoy floating in the sea. Or it's a bit like Kandinsky who said: 'The more yellow you put into a painting the less you see' . . . and again, it's like your impression of light when you compare stark opposites, eg go to a Christmas shopping scene in a big city with all the shops lit up, with all the decorations, and you see far less light than if you go to the Scottish Highlands when it's totally black, and see a light shining from a solitary cottage. It's the power of the minimal which comes out.

One does not compare Turner and Constable, and nor is it possible to compare the bindings of Ivor Robinson and Philip Smith. They stand at opposite ends of the spectrum – although it can be said that the work of the former consists of variations on the same theme, while Smith's work takes widely varying forms. It is often that bustling activity, symbolic even when illustrative, that generates the tremendous energy of the binding. And because he is always looking for new perspectives, he comes up with a number of technical innovations. They include unusual applications of leather. The first, developed during 1959, was the use of the 'feathered' onlay, originally discovered by accident. This is a slight paring of leather which when carefully glued to a 'solid' piece of coloured leather produces a blurred and indefinite edge – a marked change from the sharpness of the normal outlines – opening up a new means for the expression of mood. In the same way that Mansfield's 'moulding' of leather was suspected initially, because no one had yet thought of exploiting the natural qualities of leather (forgetting that it is, after all, as malleable and expressive as human skin), no binder until then would conceive of using 'imperfect' bits of leather any more than a carpenter would use wood-shavings. But Smith was using leather in the decorative rather than structural sense, like paint on canvas. Indeed when he sent his first feathered-onlay binding to Major J. R. Abbey, the reaction from this leading collector and authority on fine binding was a note to the effect that *he* thought it was painted.

It would be wrong to think of Smith in terms of 'gadgets' and the like, because his approach has always encompassed the art as a whole:

When one begins to see the enormous potential of how the book surfaces and even its shape can be transformed, a myriad of ideas for its extension come to mind. One has to work pretty 'urgently' and compulsively to try to manifest just a tiny percentage of these ideas. This is why for me almost every book is a new challenge and an opportunity to experiment further. It is a form of research – making prototypes to test this and that alternative structure and image. Some of them don't come off, a few succeed, but all have different intentions behind them and cannot be judged by the same criteria.

There are only a few experimentalists in every field – opening up new ground; they throw out seeds which the less creatively original workers pick up and develop. The purists, some traditionalists, who say that there is only one way to do it properly, naturally feel threatened and object that their precious domain is being perverted, contaminated by wrong ideas and so forth.

Many bookbinders find a particular formula which works well, sells well, by which they are recognised, and stick to a life of variants on that theme; it is certainly a way to keep life simple and not have to make too much effort. This to me is a mechanical way to work. On the other hand, real works of art . . . real innovations, are unpredictable and unexpected; and take long periods to digest.

Bearing in mind the flexibility of leather, it is surprising that more importance is not attached to the 'feel' of a binding, as opposed to its visual appeal – either in the conventional form, or as an art object. One of the most dramatic breaks with tradition in recent years has been achieved by Jean de Gonet, mentioned earlier. The photographs of de Gonet's bindings, while giving a perfectly valid idea of his style, inevitably lack the extra dimension that makes their 'live' appearance so effective. However, they do enable us to see what he considers the most important feature – the relationship between spine and boards through the sewing, which gives the book its characteristic form and function. It is the bands, or occasionally leather thongs and the threads around them that provide the focus of attention.

De Gonet's unusual approach provides another of those surprising coincidences that crop up in the arts since, indirectly, he shares with a very different binder, Bruce Schnabel, a fascination for the Pompidou Centre in Paris. While de Gonet may not be paying the same sort of tribute to the visible features of building construction, the similarity in concept is very apparent. It is also an intriguing thought that both binders, rebelling against the pretentiousness of design, are among the most modern practitioners in style, yet both are able to bind period books. Again, because this is his central theme, and he is not interested in achieving a different character for each book, de Gonet's choice of what each cover shall be comes down to a personal preference for certain visual effects, colours and materials – and what he does with those materials.

Like Mansfield, a 'pioneer' in the offbeat approach to leather, de Gonet is fascinated by building on what is natural – which means the inclusion of flaws and blemishes. But because their philosophies are very

Jean de Gonet's 'designs' are based on the structure of the book, and
feature the cords – though the style varies from what appears to be
basic to the elegantly sophisticated. *Antoni Tapies*, by Jean Daive
was bound (1977) in brown calf partially oxidised and waxed, with
the exposed cords laced into three pieces of the same leather onlaid.
The 'fasteners' are small pieces of corrugated calf, highlighted with
splashes of red, black and white.

76

different, his treatment of the leather involves the use of sophisticated techniques of which Mansfield would probably not have approved, eg buffing and dyeing, and to get a polished finish, even selective sand-blasting to follow regular or random configurations.

Another binder unafraid to experiment with leather, Trevor Jones, responds to de Gonet's approach thus:

Bindings used to be influenced by decoration. In the past, it was whatever the particular mode happened to be – interior decoration or architectural design, if you like – but bindings were always just decorative. When painting and sculpture became abstract in the twentieth century and we began to get bindings that were influenced by art rather than by decoration, and as art moved away from abstraction and naturalism became respectable again, it produced a dilemma for the binder whose designs are based on art, or are thought of in art terms. You either became an illustrator, producing pictures on the front of books, or you were influenced by something else. De Gonet is a binder who is influenced by binding rather than by painting or decoration, and it is the structure of the book that he is using to make the design – and that is very interesting.

Undoubtedly, de Gonet has made a major statement although one wonders whether his new path is, in fact, a cul-de-sac. There may be a limit to the number of variations possible on the one theme, compared with those open to a binder such as Ivor Robinson, who is able to produce an infinite variety of experience on the same concept. An altogether more versatile binder, the Czech Jiri Hadlač, also incorporates structural changes, but as part of a series of innovations adding up to a significant whole. One is in sewing the sheets together, and letting the cords protrude inside the covers where they are fixed, to remain part of the artistic make-up of the endpaper. (The principle is not all that far removed from what Douglas Cockerell once said about the lacing-in, far from being unsightly, it indeed made a good starting off point for decoration.)

However, to return to Trevor Jones (and there are similarities in style between him and Hadlač, dissimilar as they are in most ways), his interest in scraps of odd leather is a feature of his attitude towards design, but he will be remembered more for his *treatment* of leather. He was, for example, the first British binder to use dyes, seeing them as an extension of the range of possibilities for the experimental binder. Jones shares Edgar Mansfield's regard for the natural qualities of leather, and the application of spirit-stain leather dyes – varying in effect from delicate tinting to bold contrasts – in no way conflicts with this attitude.

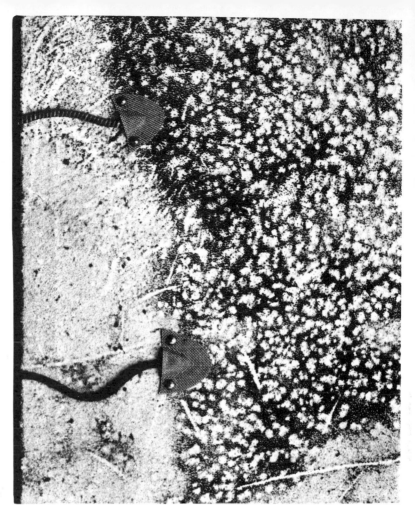

In what might almost seem a protest at the inflexibility of the traditional book, Jean de Gonet's 1980 binding of *Un Divertissement* by Franz Kafka has covers in a particularly supple calf, to match the extended exposed cords fastened by flexible metal rivets.

The two main methods of working with dye are stencilling and a resist method similar to batik as used in textiles. One of his most impressive innovations was in the resist technique. He began in the conventional manner by drawing linear patterns of Cow Gum rubber solution directly from the tube on to the leather. The solution, when dry, resists the dye and can then be peeled cleanly away. The resist can be removed selectively, and further areas drawn in for subsequent overlays of dye. The only comparable technique was that of Brazilian bookbinder Ursula Katzenstein, who applied her design on slightly dampened leather with hot wax before brushing on the dye. Although he had done something similar on cloth, Jones was cautious about using hot wax on leather; he suspected it might darken the skin, and be difficult to remove completely after use. An alternative to the Cow Gum has been a latex adhesive which has the advantage of being opaque white when applied, rather than transparent, so it is more easily visible when marking out the design.

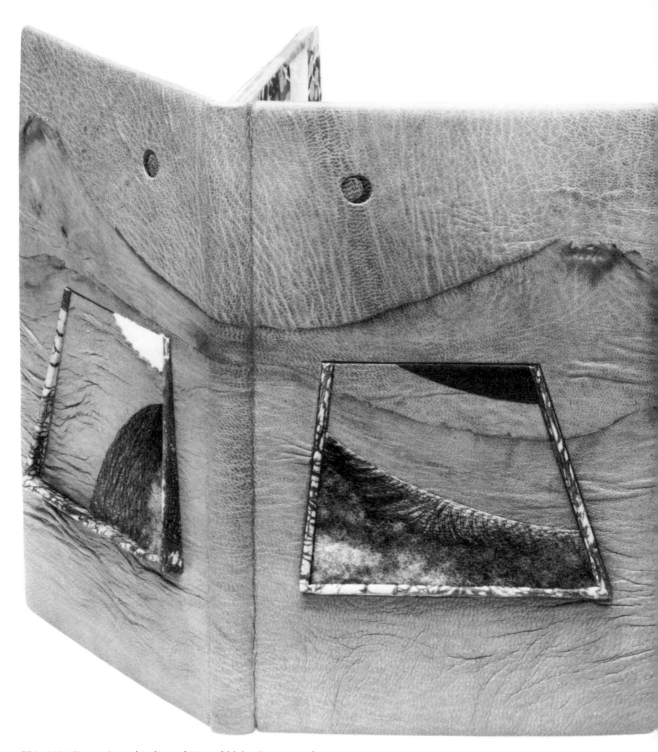

This 1980 Trevor Jones binding of *Winterfold*, by George Mackay Brown, makes use of the natural contours of the goatskin as stand-in for landscapes. Three part-skins are scarf-jointed together to make the cover, and the sheepfold is constructed of plywood covered in glove leather with craquelé dye marks. The design was influenced by a book of photographs of Orkney stone structures seen from the air. The Jacob's sheep fleece inlay is intended to be reminiscent of both sheep and the seashore: the skin of the fleeces tones to a bright blue from the greys and browns of the wool.

78

But his break-through came with the substitution of a flour paste ('paperhanger's paste') for the rubber or latex solutions. Mixed as a thick cream, it is painted on areas of the leather, then left to dry. The advantage is that if the leather is smooth-surfaced – without a pronounced grain, like calf or kid – it can be flexed or pulled to crack the paste. This cracking can be controlled to give a particular scale of texture or directional emphasis, so that the dye when applied shows up only in the cracks. Jones has pasted whole gloves, then inserted his hand when the paste was dry, and opened and closed his fist before brushing on the dye. However, the flour resist has also been used without a craquelé effect, in his 1983 version of *The Amazons* (see illustration), in combination with stencils.

Having made comparisons between Jones and Jiri Hadlač it is interesting that the Czech binder has used dye on sheets of hand-made paper inside a book to create abstract compositions (eg to provide an atmospheric background for the text of a story that requires it, such as Edgar Allen Poe's *The Raven*.) It is particularly effective when he has copied the text by hand, and perhaps incorporated the loose cords.

Much of Jones' work is admired by Edgar Mansfield, despite the fact that the use of dyes *could* be said to interfere with the natural qualities of the leather (something Jones denies). But there are a number of binders who work on leather in ways Mansfield would not have approved. Ivor Robinson uses another painting analogy:

Ben Nicholson, of the St Ives School of painters, used to say you couldn't hear the seagulls in St Ives because the painters were so busy scratching their surfaces. They were doing this in the '30s and '40s, and now people have decided they are going to attack this precious surface – leather – and attack its surface by glass papering and staining, and so on.

This does not apply to most outstanding binders, those featured here, although admittedly de Gonet's work has a distinctively refined finish – but his motivation is different from most. In any case, though Mansfield's leather philosophy is difficult to contest, there are of course no absolute truths in the arts. David Sellars, recognising both sides of the coin, explains his own attitude: 'I strongly believe that leather is *the* medium for binding and I always try to use it – but not so that I can't manipulate it to make my personal statement. It is the expressive nature of the materials that I try to bring out, and this might mean using glass paper. I don't touch the grain, but rub down the high

areas around it – the parts that would otherwise have a high gloss, plastic-like finish.'

Among those who prefer not to feature leather exclusively are Jan Sobota, an expatriate Czech, and Daniel Knoderer, of France: very different binders in their approach, yet both with a fondness for the sculptural form and for mixing leather with more unconventional materials. Sobota is one of the most original of the front-rank binders, and the wide range of his work ensures a broader appeal. His modern design bindings vary from the illustrative to the symbolic and even to structural novelties within the conventional parameters, and he also produces what might broadly be called free-standing pieces, in a variety of guises as illustrated in this book. Most of these are containers for the bound book – a development of the slipcase or even the dust-jacket. The Czech edition of Tolkien's *The Hobbit* (1980–81), for example, is supported by a piece of sculpture in character, made from pulpboard and balsa wood covered in black and natural calf and white pigskin; *The Man With the Cowboy Heart*, by Jack Schafer (1981), is framed in its container – a plastic case with open front. The cowboy's hat is black, the casing itself is in black and natural calf, and the book inside is bound in reversed cowhide with onlays in two shades of red.

The novelties which followed are delightful. *The Tree of Knowledge* (1982) is a small 'bookcase' for five philosophical books, published separately by a Prague publisher. The tree is made of pasteboard, with plexiglass cases – which can be opened to remove the books – at the ends of the branches; it is covered with sheepskin. The books (7 × 7cm) have calf spines and back covers; the front covers are of special paper (also handmade by Sobota) with tiny fragments of natural items – butterfly, leaf, blossom, bird feather, and cut fruit – fed in as it is made from the pulp. The paper is coated with plastic film as protection.

The Apple Tree of Cobweb Threads, by Jaroslav Seifert (1982) is a long poem about thoughts of love and natural beauty that come while sitting under an apple tree. The case is made of laminated paper covered with calf and painted. The book pages are of hand-made paper, each hand-painted as an apple slice; the pen-and-ink drawing and lettering are also by Sobota.

The most intriguing, in my opinion, is *Cinderella* (1982), represented by a silk dress fit for a princess (it actually fits a small girl), and a walnut made of laminated paper covered with wrinkled calfskin and painted. The inside of the nut is gold leaf with a little red paint to produce a patina. The text is silk-screened on the dress in brown, and this folds into the nut.

What the traditionalists who object to a decoration

(above)   *The Tree of Knowledge*, by Jan Sobota

(below)   *The Apple Tree of Cobweb Threads*, by Jan Sobota

Cinderella, by Jan Sobota

encroaching from the front cover on to the spine, and even across the back, would make of Knoderer's *Hé*, by Michel Butor-Baltazar (1981), on which the title runs off the surface altogether, I cannot imagine. The book itself is constructed in the traditional way, with the binding in various pastel shades of morocco leather. However, the large letters of the title are made from polyester sheet, cut out, textured and glued together – after which they are screwed to the book covers. It is difficult to see whether the letters are metal, painted wood, leather or plastic, and it is of course partly Knoderer's intention to surprise us.

Some of Knoderer's marriages of leather and other materials, such as metal, are more controversial, because there is some difference of opinion as to whether leather joints will stand up to the unfamiliar strain of supporting heavy metal and similar pieces. Although Knoderer is an experimenter, however, his background in the traditional craft is impeccable, and he seldom shows anything new without a comprehensive study of all the issues. Another original idea is to reverse roles with the author (in this case his friend Michel Butor), because there is now an imbalance, he feels, between the two roles – the inside of the book needing to be changed in the same proportion as the outside. The opportunity lies in presenting him with a blank book already bound and decorated, but needing some form of literary content. His motivation is that authors, like binders, are inhibited by classical presentation – the traditional sameness of typography, with conventional layout and plates in set positions. Since writers are accustomed to freedom in their poetic images and style, they should be given scope to explore new methods of presentation. The results should be interesting.

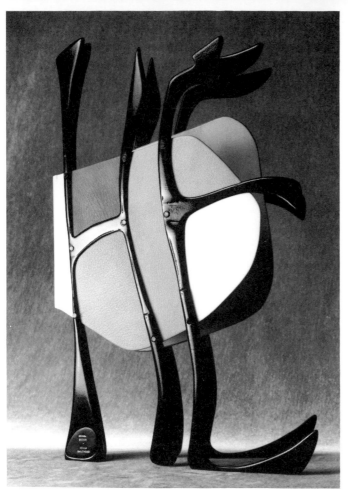

Hé, bound by Daniel Knoderer

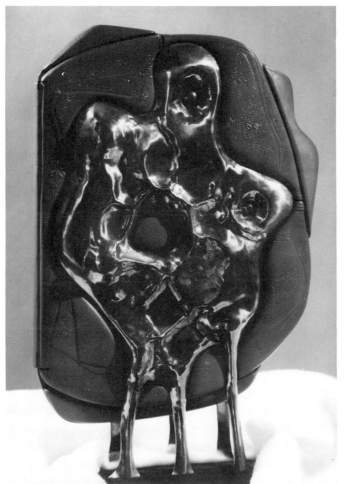

Chronique des Astéroïdes by Michael Butor. Knoderer has made the book a freestanding piece of sculpture. The binding is in cyclamen calf with some intricate gilding, and the metal attachment is studded with amethysts. Note the irregular edges of the covers.

6

OUT IN FRONT:
PHILIP SMITH AND IVOR ROBINSON

An increasing awareness of creative binding will continue to stimulate demand. At present it is difficult for binders, like others in the arts, to make a decent living from their skills; almost all need to supplement their income from teaching, or conservation and restoration work. A tiny minority are on the verge of taking the plunge to bind full-time; others are confident of survival if they did, but would not want the pressure of committing themselves totally to such a creatively demanding taskmaster. One of the few who has successfully made the break is Philip Smith, of Merstham, Surrey, England.

I referred earlier to Philip Smith as 'arguably' the outstanding binder of the past quarter of a century. Any doubt is because, although he is universally respected for his talent, and what he has done for modern binding, there are some who find his work overpowering. Smith stands out not only for the brilliance of his work, in craftsmanship no less than design, but for the challenging way he has established parameters, stimulating – or provoking – others to strive for higher standards, whether in admiration of his work, or in reaction against it. His influence in raising the status of hand binding has flowed partly through his writing and lecturing, educating those who remain suspicious of the modern approach, and partly through his decision to fix his fees in line with those paid for other crafts. Roger Powell, his teacher and main critic, does at least give Smith credit for persuading collectors to pay reasonable prices for bindings. Ironically, because he charges on an hourly basis – the norm in most professions, but unusual in the arts – and because his bindings are thoroughly researched, intricate and take much time to execute, he has virtually priced himself out of the market in Britain, apart from a few dedicated collectors. His best work goes to the USA; British museums and university libraries can afford only his student work and very early examples, not representative of the last twenty years.

Despite being gentle-natured and generous in offering help and advice, there are no half-measures in anything Philip Smith says or does; he cannot compromise over what he believes to be 'right' and 'wrong'. The result is that it is impossible to be indifferent to his work. Some people dislike certain features, while admiring the ideas and technical expertise. It would be difficult, though, for anyone who appreciates fine craftsmanship not to be moved by some quality or other in something in his range of work. Yet his output is not large for a full-time craftsman, as some of his bindings take up to a couple of years to complete.

Smith came to bookbinding by accident, and although his subsequent career followed a definable pattern it has been influenced by 'a network of people and events'. It is not only the big events, of course, that manipulate our lives; small chance encounters can have far-reaching effects and casual remarks can lead to the solution of a longstanding problem. The difference between success and failure can be the ability to catch these threads and be alive to their significance. The 'accident' was in 1957 at art school in Southport, where he had enrolled with the not uncommon ambition of becoming a painter or sculptor. Because he found shop-bought sketchbooks expensive, and not durable enough for his requirements, he asked the lecturer in bookbinding if he might mess about in spare moments to assemble his own pads. But he was told that the equipment was in constant use; the only way he could get access was to take bookbinding as part of his course – one of the craft subjects being necessary for the Intermediate Course in Arts & Crafts. Binding was not the one he would have chosen, but he joined that class for the sake of expediency. Indeed, although his tutor provided the right grounding, being a stickler for high technical standards, Philip Smith's progress was unspectacular, and it was partially ignorance of what was expected which led him to try an experimental approach to the two set bindings required for his exam.

If you examine the bindings done by a number of

students on art/craft courses, you are often impressed by the freshness and ingenuity some display – although there is a gulf between these inspired but essentially amateurish efforts and what they could be expected to produce much later, if they continued binding. Smith's exam bindings obviously came into this category. They featured pen and watercolour drawings on the edges; faces which smiled when the edges were fanned out, and tall narrow houses which grew wider – all the influences of art superficially applied to the craft aspect. But it was enough to bring them to the attention of Roger Powell, assessor to the Department of Education, who was at the time teaching at the Royal College of Art.

Although Smith did not have the qualifications necessary at the time to gain admission to the Royal College, Powell was sufficiently impressed to pull a few strings. (So much for any impression given that Powell was a reactionary who had no time for originality.) When he embarked on his three-year course, Smith intended to switch back to art at the first opportunity, but at the Royal College he began to get some indication of the medium's potential, and soon became bitten by the bookbinding bug. He could not help being impressed, for example, by the expertise of Bernard Middleton, who was then technical assistant for bookbinding, and by the work and ideas of Peter Waters who had already been on the course for two years, and was the only other student for most of Smith's stay. He considers he learnt more from Waters (who was to become a partner in Roger Powell's bindery) than anyone at the time, especially as Powell was only on hand one day a week.

After leaving the Royal College, Smith taught full-time at Malvern while he tried to develop his binding skills, and in two years he had time to complete only one that might be considered creative – G. D. Hobson's *English Bindings Before 1500*, which won the prestigious Thomas Harrison Binding Competition, for students and inexperienced binders. In 1957, shortly afterwards, he joined Sydney Cockerell as chief assistant, remaining in that important workshop for two years. While at Letchworth he was one of four binders asked to submit designs for a Prayer Book to be presented by the Duke of Edinburgh to a Royal Naval chapel in Sydney, Australia; and with the publicity associated with the resulting competition, supported by a one-day-a-week teaching job, he was able to set up on his own in 1960. (The reason that so many binders leave interesting positions to set up on their own has less to do with ego than the desire to develop their own style of work. A good example was the decision some years ago of Ivor Robinson to get

(right) This limited edition of Gogol's *The Overcoat* was bound (1976) by Trevor Jones, in vellum, an unusual medium for him. The markings on the pathway, across the lower part of the book, began as an emphasis of the natural spine markings on the vellum. The overcoat was designed as a fully three-dimensional coat with fur collar, belt, cape and buttons – made up from a scaled-down paper pattern derived from books of historical costume, in grey leather with darker leather lining, sewn on an old treadle sewing-machine. The box, made a year later, was also sewn, in a wool-mixture cloth with accessories.

(overleaf left) *Gigi*, by Colette, was bound by Bernard Middleton, in 1979, in red goatskin, inlaid with black, and tooled in gold and black to create a warm and feminine design.

(overleaf below left) Jacqueline Liekens's 1981 binding for *La Crevette dans tous ses Etats*, by François Ponge, won the prize of the Ministère des Classes Moyennes at the Rotary Club exhibition in Brussels. Bound in sand-coloured levant morocco, the design is created with old rose levant morocco and brown box-calf onlays, curved lines tooled in blind, and small lead balls. The doublures and flyleaves are in brown box-calf, and the endpapers of hand-painted Kromekote paper.

(overleaf right) Most fine bindings of *Finnegan's Wake* endeavour to find answers to some of the questions James Joyce has posed in the book. Philip Smith has in this one (1981–2) gone for several. His sculptured surfaces are built from balsa wood, the polystyrene skeleton fleshed out with epoxy putty covered with leather, puckered and modelled. The title on the book takes the form of an anagram: *Jaycem Jones Fake (CHapEL) Winsagen*, with a subtitle on the box and the usual name on the additional casket. The figure on the cover suggests both decay and rebirth, and Smith felt it must therefore be three-dimensional in the sculptural sense, to express this ambiguity. Is the giant decaying or is it reintegrating? It is both. The eyes, made of abalone shell, are awake. Move the book and life is apparently there, as eight ball-bearings in the hollow skull (thoughts) recycle continuously. The crocodile strap alongside is a comment on the river theme.

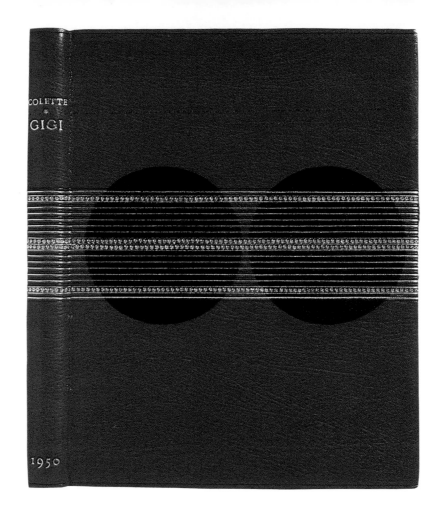

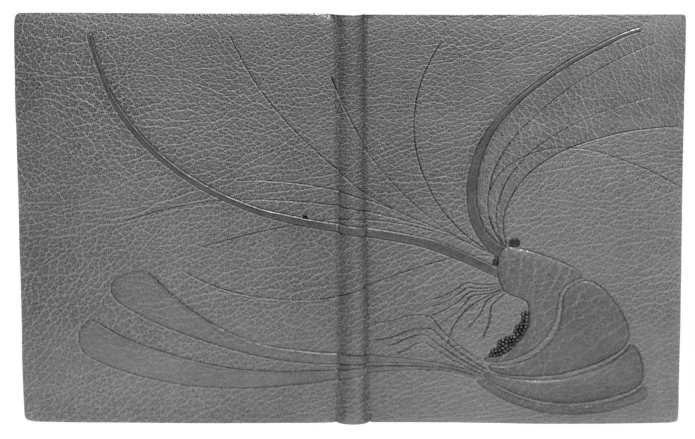

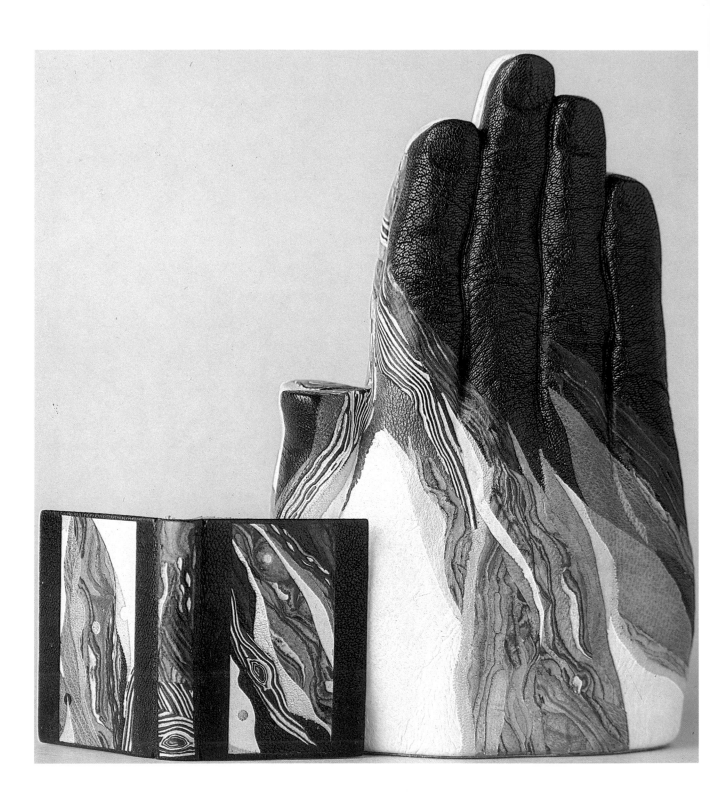

(left) A hand 6½in high, modelled from his own hand (without the thumb), forms Philip Smith's case for a miniature edition of Robert Louis Stevenson's *Prayers Written at Vailima*. Designed as a piece of sculpture, the hand is made from balsa wood covered in leather.

(above) For this huge edition of *Macbeth*, one of Philip Smith's designs features Macbeth; the other a castle, symbolising power, with three witches in the foreground and soldiers by the walls. When Smith first experimented with the strips he discovered that the background was lost, so he modified the design. When he was satisfied, the covers were completed in leather and then cut into strips. To complement the effect, the page edges are striped in gold and palladium, and the first flyleaf is in two shades of red suede.

away from Edgar Mansfield, a fellow-lecturer at the London College of Printing – someone he very much admired, but whose strong views would have continued to be an influence he would need to shake off if he was to 'do his own thing'.)

The next phase was significant. In a feature article, 'An Autobiography of Indebtedness', in the first issue (1981) of *The New Bookbinder* (journal of the Designer Bookbinders), Philip Smith wrote about this period when, having acquired the basic skills of the craft, it had become a matter of developing imagination in terms of the medium.

Skills and imagination are really inseparable from creative work; imagination gives life to it, and skill, the intelligent servant, prevents the chaos of un-channelled imagination. To harness the two in productive work, a discriminating intellect is required to sort out just those elements helpful in achieving the goal . . .

Recent neuro-physiological research has demons-trated that the intuitive or 'poetic' side of one's nature – which faces inwards – is mediated by the right hemisphere of the brain, but this tends to be drowned by the flood of concerns falling on to the more dominant logic-orientated half – which deals with the outer world. In order to bring about a proper partnership of the two it is necessary to find a systematic way to quieten the noisier side. The most important piece in my jig-saw was given to me when in 1960 a very good friend of ours introduced us to a psychological method designed to enable a busy working person to develop inner tranquillity. In retrospect, the spin-off from this practice is very noticeable in the changes in my work which began about this time . . .

My work became less 'head-orientated' and more spontaneous. In my own time I began to experiment with feathered onlays combined with stamping in gold and blind. At last the old influences seemed to have been assimilated and I was working on asymmetrical and freely drawn images.

In 1966 Sydney Cockerell was approached by Anthony Fair of Sotheby's book department, who wanted to start a collection of modern English bindings; Smith was one of the craftsmen recommended. One of the first books given to him to bind was the Ganymed Press edition of *King Lear*, mentioned earlier, and which Smith acknowledges as a turning point in his career. It was, incidentally, one of his first bindings to try to 'interpenetrate' the book, by having Lear's face on the front cover, the back of his

head on the back cover, with the implication that the book in between was his brains, or mind, and the drama of his life; in other words, the binding was not merely decoration (although superb on that level alone), but used the book, physically and psychologically, to make up the total book-art object.

Following Designer-Bookbinder exhibitions touring the United States in 1971 and 1972, Smith's work found a natural market – particularly through the enthusiasm and support of Mel Kavin, head of one of the largest Californian binderies and former President of the Library Binding Institute of the USA, and other leading figures on the American scene. The next milestone was the 'book walls' project, described earlier, but there were others, including his five volume bindings in 1977–8 of the beautiful Cobden-Sanderson *Doves Bible* of 1905. Smith offsets its remarkable simplicity with a contrastingly vivid but harmonious landscape effect, depicting the Creation in five separate visual images. For a period Smith emphasised the binding's sculptural form, and this included the use of detachable 'follies', such as a headpiece in the shape of peaked mountains for Tolkien's *The Silmarillion*. He also made an aesthetically pleasing container for a miniature copy of Robert Louis Stevenson's *Prayers Written at Valima*: it was made from balsa wood and epoxy resin, and covered in leather.

In my view, the other outstanding binder of today is Ivor Robinson, of Trindles, Oxford. His work, as already said, is utterly different from that of Philip Smith, and his views are in some respects – not all – diametrically opposed. To choose another Englishman may seem parochial, but it is not done casually. Much of the work done in France or the USA in the past twenty-five years has been pleasing, but individuals do not stand out.

There is, in any case, some controversy about the standards of craftsmanship in France, a general acceptance of the fact that leathers traditionally pared too thinly tend to make the hinges fragile; yet another body of opinion that this is offset by the excellence of other aspects of the craft. It is difficult to make direct comparisons because the two schools have always had different objectives; the French going for finesse and the British for durability and proper functioning. Within the necessarily narrow parameters of what is 'best', a panel of experts might decide that some French bindings showed slightly greater precision; they might equally feel they were *too* perfect.

Sally Lou Smith, an American who trained and has done all of her binding in England, and is recognised by her colleagues and collectors as a major talent, is one

SOME OUTSTANDING FRENCH BINDERS

Some impressive bindings have been produced in France during the past half-century. I have already given credit to Pierre Legrain as a major influence on the new wave of the 1930s, and acknowledged the debt to Paul Bonet, who is better known because of his large output (having experimented with many artistic styles, such as fauvism, cubism and surrealism). Even if we share the concern of such experts as Jean de Gonet at the profusion of spectacular abstract design that he inspired, he and some of those of the next generation have played major roles in the development of modern binding. This section is a small tribute to some of them.

Fairly typical of Paul Bonet's ability to capture our immediate attention is this design of 1952 for *Jazz* by Matisse. The mosaic decoration of various inlaid calf leathers might have intimidated a craftsman-binder, but the colours and design are inspired by the Matisse illustrations inside the book.

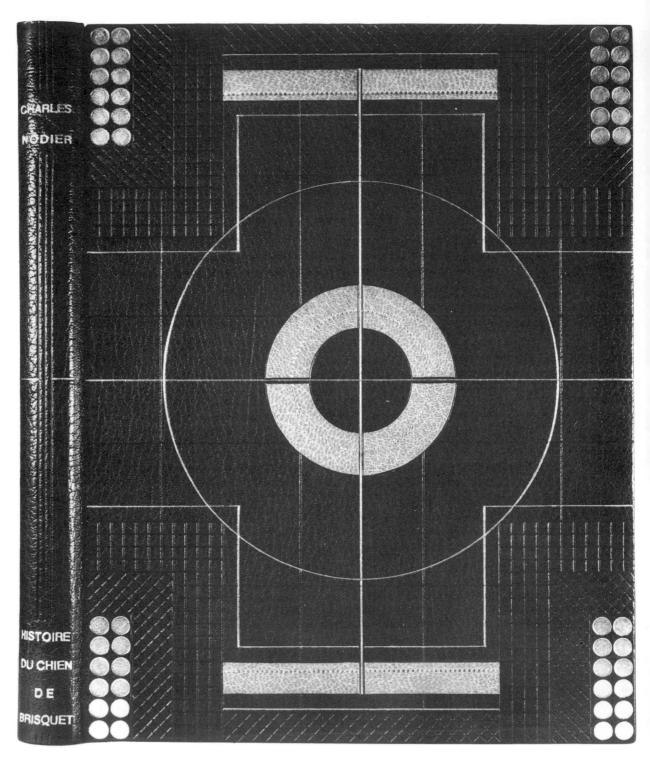

Circles are predominant in many Pierre Legrain designs. This large book *Histoire Du Chien de Brisquet*, by Charles Nodier, was bound in 1950 by his son-in-law, J. Anthoine-Legrain, after a design by Legrain. Anthoine adopted the famous name when he took over his father-in-law's bindery. The binding is in dark-blue morocco with fawn onlays, and gold and blind tooling. The doublures are of dark-blue silk.

who admires the quality of French binding but wonders whether designers (from Bonet down) can really make as significant a contribution as the craftsman-artist who conceives and executes his or her own work. 'Ideas come to me from working with the materials I use. It beats me how designers can come up with ideas, when they are not used to working with those materials.'

Furthermore, nearly all bindings from France (technically accomplished, or not) are the products of a team effort, which makes it doubly difficult to single out individuals. The relationship can sometimes be almost mechanical too – very different from the natural collaboration of Bruce Schnabel and his fellow artists, which is more a group effort than a compartmentalised operation of specialists working on the same project. This chapter, however, is concerned with individual excellence.

Rose Adler, one of the few French binders who designed her own bindings – and one of the main inspirations of Jean de Gonet – produced *Cirque de L'Etoile Filante*, by Georges Roualt, in 1951. Dark- and light-grey morocco, with white and blind tooling set in the relatively plain background. The mosaic star on the front cover has six colours.

And Robinson's work provides a complete contrast to that of Philip Smith. While Smith produces so much evidence of change, it could be said that Robinson is in a rut – until such time as he finds another technique or style that interests him; but the quality of his design is such that his many admirers will not complain if he never changes. And this, after all, is what really matters. Philosophies will come and go, but in the final analysis – as Douglas Cockerell suggested – a well-crafted binding will always be judged by its appearance.

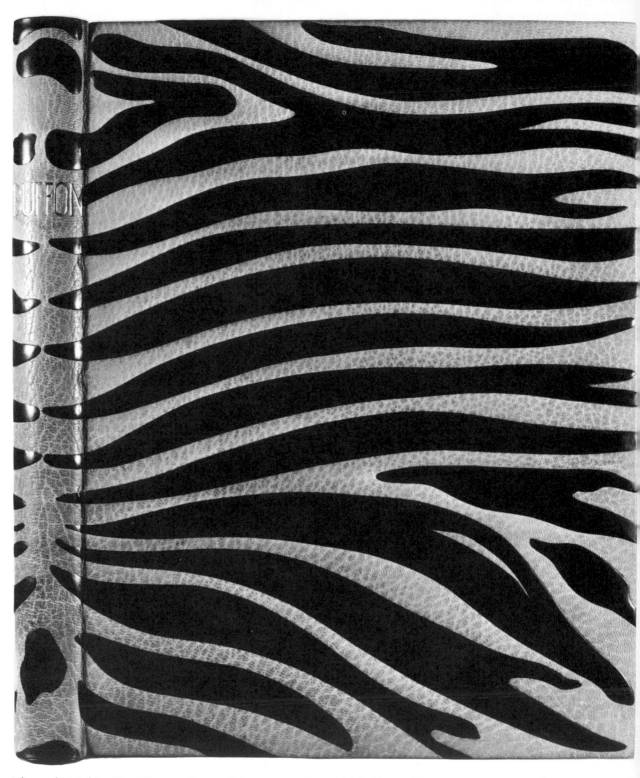

(*above and top right*)   Henri Creuzevault, one of the most versatile of French binders, usually projected the theme of the book in his design. But the feature of Verlaine's *Parallelement* is a series of erotic lithographs by Pierre Bonnard, and he appears to have played safe by concentrating on the title *(top right)*. The gold and blind parallel lines are tooled on pink morocco, and the endpapers are in pink watered silk (c 1940). In contrast is the 1949 'zebra' binding *(above)* designed and executed by him for Picasso, *Eaux-Fortes Originales Pour des Textes De Buffon*.

(*right*)   *Enorme Figure De La Désse Raison* by André Frenaud, designed by Pierre Lucian Martin in 1963, is one of the most spectacular bindings to be seen of any period or 'school'. Bound in black, grey and white morocco with onlays in box calf in similar colours, the design creates an optical illusion of enormous depth. Unfortunately lost in the photograph is some unusual gilt lettering on the spine.
(*The six French bindings by courtesy of the Victoria & Albert Museum*)

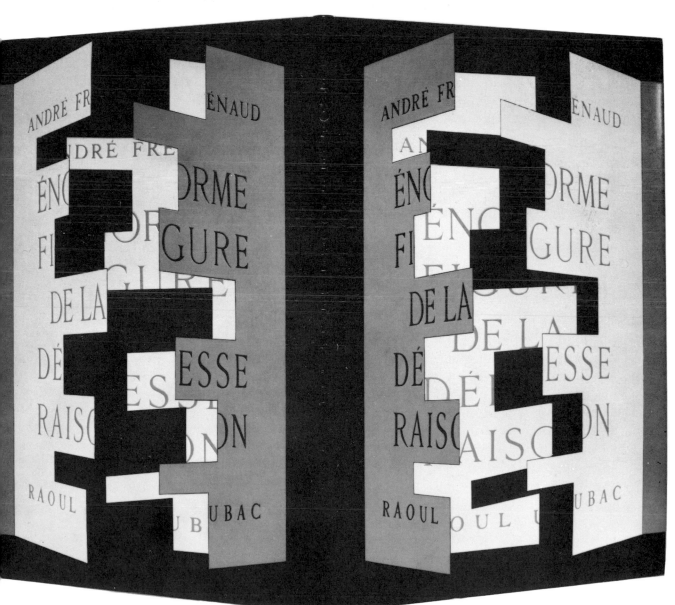

Ivor Robinson does not bind full-time – mainly because he enjoys teaching and contact with the fresh, uncluttered minds of young artists. As part of a visual-arts degree course at Oxford Polytechnic, for example, he changed the title of his bookbinding course to 'Book Works', to encompass the different experiences brought to the study by students of photography, textile design, etc. At the college he has been senior lecturer in Bookbinding and Design studies since 1959; Visual Studies Field Chairman since 1980. Before that he was at the London College of Printing and Graphic Arts (alongside Edgar Mansfield) and at Salisbury College of Art, but his reputation has brought him appointments as guest lecturer to overseas bodies. He was trained at Bournemouth College of Art.

Robinson's technical expertise was never in question from his days as a prizewinning student, and in the 1950s his work was already being exhibited internationally and he was receiving his first commissions. It was not until he settled for his current style – featuring gold tooling on black or brown leather – that he traversed the divide between the very good and the outstanding. It is impossible for the casual observer, impressed by the relationship between design and leather, to appreciate the intricacy of the gold tooling, which looks simple but is laboriously worked, millimetres at a time. (Many binders avoid gold tooling because of its difficulty, and might benefit from learning, through their mistakes if necessary, to use it properly.) In Ascona, Switzerland, in 1971 he was Silver Medallist and Double Bronze Medallist in the Prix Paul Bonet International Competition.

His bindings are housed in important institutional and private collections all over the world, although he is perhaps better known in Europe, particularly Scandinavia and Germany, than in the United States. He was one of the few foreigners invited to become a member of the German binders' guild, the Meister der Einbandkunst. He is the author of *Introducing Bookbinding* (1968 and 1984).

At first glance it might seem that Robinson's designs are variations on a theme; in fact they are variations on three themes, all symbols which fascinate him and provide the inspiration for the basic drawing he uses for his design. These are: landscapes, helmets and the crucifixion – all evident in the illustrations used here. There is a common link in the interlocking of shapes, particularly noticeable in the landscapes, although if one takes the helmet – with the nose-piece being the positive, the eye-piece the negative, and reversible – the same effect is experienced.

He uses these themes to illustrate his argument against the naivety of trying to interpret the author's text. Reverting to Dante, he asks: 'How many words are there in Dante; how many concepts are there? What can you do on a book cover by claiming that you're starting out to interpret? Why not go for what you can do? Which is to relate to the form of the book, which is a constructed landscape.'

What is remarkable about Robinson's work is that an inspirational pencil drawing, ostensibly no more than a doodle, can contain such significance that it will match the character of the book for which it is chosen as though conceived for it.

7
THE NAMES TO NOTE

Note: The works of the binders listed below are housed in private collections all over the world. Many owners wish to remain anonymous, and in any case they are too numerous to list here. I have, however, given the names of major museums or libraries where bindings might, in certain circumstances, be inspected.

James Brockman, Headington, Oxford, England
Conservation and restoration enable Brockman to work in his bindery full-time, with a full-time assistant, and also to continue his learning process, throwing up ideas which can be used in creative binding. Jim Brockman is a versatile and superb craftsman who, unfairly, is too often identified with the novelty of his metal/electronic bindings. They are so ingenious, however, that it would be a serious omission not to describe *Beauty and Deformity* (1979) in some detail.

Embarking on this, his second electronic 'adventure', Brockman had a wide choice of subject matter available. The only prerequisite was in its physical form – it had to be at least 40mm thick, to allow boards of 9mm housing the electronic 'works' and moving parts. His ultimate choice was *Theory on the Classification of Beauty and Deformity* (1815) by Mary Schimmelpenninck, an unusual study of human characteristics and personalities, with plates and charts comparing human profiles with those of animals. It seemed to him a suitably strange book for a strange binding.

Because the nature of an electronic binding is that its various functions should be operational – in this case to provide changes of image and mood – the 'controls' are necessarily linked to the front cover, irrespective of other clever effects elsewhere. Jim Brockman explains:

Eight sub-titles were taken from charts in the book, four each to cover 'Beauty' and 'Deformity', and these used to label eight switches. I managed to obtain a dished flexible mirror, and eight stainless steel buttons were to be fixed around the edge. When selecting the individual sub-title, the button alongside would be pressed, lighting the red light-emitting diodes adjacent to the mirror buttons. These would then be pressed, and upon looking into the mirror one's reflection would be distorted to match the sub-title.

The rear board was to depict 'Beauty', a picture of a nude female under moving louvres only to be visible when in the open position. A silhouette depicting 'Deformity' was decided upon for the inside of the rear board.

Stainless steel was chosen for the metalwork where possible to avoid the tarnishing problems met with brass.

With his first electronic binding, the forwarding had incorporated traditional methods. But the existing binding of *Beauty and Deformity* was a poorly rebacked cloth case, which might have hinted at problems ahead. When dismantled, the spine was found to be heavily glued up, and some of the leaves water-stained, so the book had to be washed and resized. Brockman takes up the story:

Operating one of the switches of James Brockman's electronic binding for *Beauty and Deformity*.

It is crucial with any flat spine binding that there be as little swelling as possible. The thickness of the paper was measured with a micrometer and a suitable handmade paper of the exact thickness was obtained. The guards and leaves were then pared with a knife, glued together and pressed. The whole book treated in this way produced a solid text-block without swelling. After sewing, the spine was glued up to hold it square with PVA coloured with yellow acrylic paint. The edges were lightly trimmed and coloured with the same acrylic paint as the spine.

The page edges were then used for the title (with other edge decoration), drawn in Indian ink by Angela James, who was at that time working for Brockman. So was another Fellow of Designer Bookbinders, Bryan Cantle, whose general contribution was invaluable. Equally fascinating is the engineering skill required to ensure that the weighty tome still functioned as a book – that its double-acting hinges enabled the covers to be opened widely – and to incorporate the power source with eight solar panels and built-in mains charger.

Brockman is slightly embarrassed by the attention his electronic bindings have received; they have distracted attention from his main interest, working in leather. Although he was bored by his six-year apprenticeship in gold finishing, it is undoubtedly this skill that was developed by the two men who inspired him in the early days, Sydney Cockerell and Ivor Robinson. The result was a talent for gold tooling that has few equals, as my photographs show. They also illustrate how fresh and interesting his designs are. Although he has no arts training, Brockman has no objection to the designer who does not bind; he considers that someone who does not know what is possible is more likely to extend frontiers than a craftsman, who might be inhibited by what he knows. 'I continually hope to produce better bindings and look forward to each one in the hope it will be the best yet.'

Apart from his one-off commissions, in 1982–3, as Arts Fellow to the Gregynog Press, now part of the University of Wales, he designed and executed fifteen special bindings – working in the original Press bindery – of *Four Great Castles*, by Dr Arnold Taylor, with original etchings by David Woodford, and with a foreword by HRH The Prince of Wales.

Collections include: the Victoria & Albert Museum; the Lilly Library, University of Indiana; the Bridwell Library; Southern Methodist University, Dallas, Texas.

Santiago Brugalla, Barcelona, Spain
The name Brugalla is known in almost every country where hand bookbinding is considered of any importance, because Santiago is the son of a famous father, Emilio, from whom he learned the traditional skills. That apprenticeship, which began forty years ago when he was still a schoolboy, has made him one of Europe's most accomplished craftsmen. His tooling, particularly in gold and palladium, is outstanding, and although he works mainly in leather his skills enable him to manipulate it in novel ways, particularly in creating a relief style (building up the board underneath in contrast to the conventional onlay).

Working alone, frequently for eleven or twelve hours a day, Brugalla is invariably faithful to the text, usually through his design. This is neither illustrative nor symbolic, yet always in accord with the mood of the book, whether it is a contemporary publication or was produced in the eighteenth century. He has been exhibited internationally since the early 1960s, and at the Legatoria del Bel Libro at Ascona, Switzerland, in 1971 he was awarded the Prix Paul Bonet gold medal for his binding of André Gide's *Thesée*. His publications include *El Arte en el Libro y en la Encuadernacion*, Spain, 1977.

Collections include: Biblioteca Nacional de Madrid; Biblioteca de Cataluña; Humanities Research Center, University of Texas.

Lage Eric Carlson, New Haven, Connecticut, USA
One of the pictorial school, setting out to evoke 'emotions of life' which he feels require representation, Carlson uses colour vividly to enhance the three-dimensional feel of his bindings, along with the texture of the leather and grain direction. 'I use a great deal of colour mosaic pieces as positive spaces in the basic rectangular book-cover format. Equally important are the spaces between the positive spaces – the negative ones. Emotion in art is not specific and cannot be translated into words, or felt in the same way as "sad" or "gay". But I try to find the range by the use of colour and form.' It is for this reason that Carlson is attracted to poetry, which features quite strongly among his bindings.

Carlson did not take up binding by design – his initial interest was art, which led him to take a five-year Bachelor of Fine Arts degree at the University of Washington. From working part-time in the Universi-

(*above right*)   This Santiago Brugalla binding of a book illustrated by Marc Chagall shows how the influence of the artist featured in the book can be allowed to dominate the cover design.

(*right*)   Another huge binding by Santiago Brugalla (79 × 64cm or 31 × 25in), *Astres Egarés*, by Marcel Jauhandeau, features some interesting onlay work.

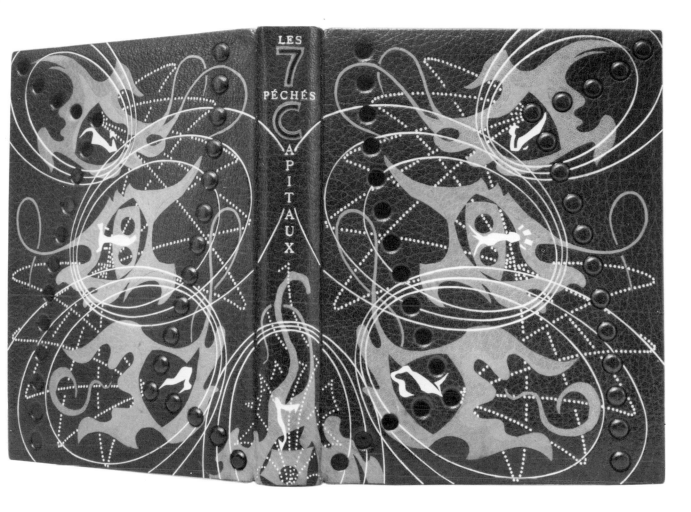

ty Library bindery, he became Conservator for the Law Library, supplementing his training with a year at the Capricornus School of Bookbinding. Later he carried out conservation and bookbinding on a contract basis for the University of California and the San Francisco Public Library. After operating his own bindery in San Francisco for four years, he moved to the East Coast where he became manager and artist-in-residence at the Creative Arts Workshop Bindery in New Haven. Used to working on his own, Carlson found an opportunity to interact on a day-to-day basis with painters, print-makers, calligraphers and other artist-craftsmen. But 80 per cent of his time is devoted to working on com-

missions, or speculative work, and 20 per cent on teaching and administration.

An innovator ('Innovation is the rejuvenator of bookbinding,' he maintains), Carlson nevertheless tends to concentrate on traditional materials – vellum as well as leathers – although often in the sculptural form. 'I examine a binding for artistic statement on the basis of balance, proportion, rhythm, perspective and feel.'

Jeff Clements, nr Newport, Gwent, Wales

A distinctive style has made Clements one of the most respected Fellows of the Designer Bookbinders (President in 1981–3). Yet although uplifted by the creative process, he is self-critical – seldom able to achieve total satisfaction from the final results, and invariably hoping that 'next time' it will be just right! However, his jaundiced view is not shared by the many collectors who have either commissioned his work or bought from exhibitions in different parts of the world.

While not exactly prolific in his output (part of his

Jeff Clements may omit a book's title if – as in this 1976 binding of a Golden Cockerell edition of *The Pilgrim Fathers*, edited by Theodore Besterman – he feels it would interfere with the design. Bound in blue oasis morocco inlaid in grey, black, brown, sienna and vermilion, Clements suggests the voyagers leaving England on the front cover and crossing the ocean to the New World. The symbolic crosses represent the numbers of sailing vessels, slightly out of alignment because of the rocking of the boats.

income has always come from teaching, and he is currently Head of Graphics at Bristol Polytechnic), Jeff Clements has produced one-off bindings steadily since the late 1950s, an average of just over three a year. On a superficial level there is an apparent similarity in much of his work – and unquestionably a common thread runs through many – but like other ostensibly more versatile binders he has over the years explored a number of styles. They appear in easily classifiable periods, each motivated by different artistic influences.

Design has been the dominating influence on his career. He gained a National Diploma at Plymouth College of Art & Design, where he was able to take lithography and bookbinding for his final exam. In 1955, Clements was given an unusual opportunity to develop this basic grounding when, although then engaged on his period of national service in the army, he was allowed to attend evening classes for a year at the Central School of Arts & Crafts. In 1957 he started work as a self-employed graphics designer and bookbinder, although it was not long before he accepted his

first teaching post as graphic-design lecturer at his old college. In the early days he did a wide range of repair and restoration work as well as creative binding, but from the late 1950s he concentrated on the latter, his particular interest at the time was Piet Mondrian, the Dutch painter (1872–1944) and his philosophy of the relationship between horizontal/vertical axes, the active and the passive. It was an influence that remained with him.

In the early 1960s, his bindings showed the influence of another passion – the landscape of Dartmoor, with its great stones and crosses (powerful

Prometheus Bound and Prometheus Unbound, Aeschylus and Shelley, two books in one, bound by Jeff Clements in 1978. Probably the culmination of his linear-form period. Again demonstrating Clements' fondness for inlay work, it depicts Prometheus bound on the front cover, symbolised by the blackness, straining against leather thongs. His freedom is represented by the light on the back cover. The influence of musical inversion is shown by the panels at the top balanced by those facing at the bottom. Some of the inlays are recessed and picked out vividly with orange acrylic paint.

images which have fired the imagination of other artist-binders, such as Ivor Robinson). A two-year break from binding (1965–7), when he returned to art, was followed by what Clements calls his 'Black Period' because all his work was in black over sculptured boards. Like so many 'new' or 'original' ideas, the move was simply a reaction against all that was garish and spectacular in modern French binding. The phase lasted a couple of years and the bindings were popular among collectors, but were no more than part of Clements' natural development. He then tried a series of 'archaic' bindings inspired by the cycladic figures of the Italian painter Campigli, freely drawn.

In recent years he has used more colour, in the form of inlays. He has always had a personal aversion to onlays, that is to sticking thinly pared leather on to a leather surface with paste; inlay, apart from its precision, also enables him to 'draw' with a knife. He has developed a visually sculptural style with the musical connotations of construction, such as inversion, counter-point, and makes symbolic (but not illustrative) reference to the book's text.

The pattern of his binding style – indicating the influences of interests in modern sculpture, painting and the process of musical form – is easy to follow over the years, but Clements' approach and his philosophy is rather more complex:

My bindings have gradually developed into a personal style – public in that one can enjoy the designs, and (with some explanation) realise the links with the text in a symbolic way – and private in that I work out an intricate ground-plan of inter-relationships between position and shape, use of colour, number of lines or sectionalised areas. It is more than likely that no one will appreciate this or even be aware that it occurs. Though the designs are specific to each title, the design process continues from book to book with themes of line or area occurring through a number of consecutive works.

How does he see his 'older' bindings, representative of different, now forsaken periods? 'Bindings are like children. It is as though they grow up and have lives of their own to lead. I remember them, sometimes with affection, but no longer feel responsible for them.'

A classicist but not a romantic, Jeff Clements' motto is 'the maximum effect with the minimum means', and this is evident from the illustration of his work reproduced in this book. His written work includes one book, *Bookbinding*, London 1963.

Collections include: British Library; Victoria & Albert Museum; Rohsska Museum, Gothenburg; Liverpool Public Library; Welsh Arts Council, Cardiff; National Library of Wales, Aberystwyth.

Timothy C. Ely, New York, NY

An artist-craftsman who has far more in common with science-fiction writers such as Asimov, Bradbury and Moorcock than any of his contemporary binders, Ely creates fictional new worlds in maps; in the eye-catching settings he gives them these have become art forms in their own right. Taking cartography to new dimensions, his fantastic maps are presented with indecipherable mathematical and word languages, pseudo-scientific diagrams and insets, and even symbols embossed in braille – the total 'package' so exquisitely drawn and assembled that they have been described as having the look and feel of an old rare book of the future.

As noted earlier, Ely took to binding because he wanted an efficient means of presenting his drawings, regarding the book as a 'looking-at' machine. In fact, he made his first 'book' – consisting of graphite on paper, stapled together, in 1961 – at the age of twelve. But having completed his art studies (he gained a BA in Drawing and Printmaking at Western Washington University in 1972, and three years later an MFA in Design at the University of Washington), he decided to learn everything he could about book production, getting early inspiration from books by Douglas Cockerell and Philip Smith. In 1981 a National Endowment for the Arts grant enabled him to study for a year in Japan (where he also investigated hand papermaking) and England, where his bookbinding teachers were David Sellars, Daphne Beaumont-Wright and Margaret Smith.

'I am very strongly motivated by ritual and myth, cartography, visionary (folly) architecture,' he says.

I sometimes develop a book around specific processes, ie drawings which throw out on guards (which can be stitched in place and folded so that a number of large illustrations each fold down to the normal book size). As the theme, ideas, content and trigger myths of the book develop, the processes and materials for binding are gathered. I am enamoured with leather, but don't see it as an end-product. I view any durable, archivally sound material as fair game so long as its use is not gratuitous. In any case, I tend to use whatever technical means I have at my fingers – gold, when appropriate, has excitement but often is too yellow. Resins, plastic, dyes and animal bones have great latitude.

Currently I am working through a 'monolith' series of books on which the surfaces are paint materials of varying viscosities; when dry and polished they resemble slate or lead. They feel very cold (which was a surprise!), and carry on the stone image from the book.

Ely is equally motivated by the environment, by images such as the rundown state of the streets of New York which he describes here:

Cracks in the tarmac are everywhere, and filled with dirt, silt, mud, water, oil, the stray earth colours are minimal but have heavy metaphoric overtones. I'm exploring tactile textures in book structures and want to create tension between the touchable and the untouchable.

I view binding as a process and rarely as a 'thing'. There are several directions currently within book art, and we as artists, thinkers, binders have many resources – the processes used in conservation can lend a tool towards amplifying specific expressions. It feels continually important to be functionally aware of the traditional and contemporary practices and to unite these with the visual reflections (however autobiographical) of the painted or printed pages.

Deborah Evetts, New York, NY

English born and trained, Deborah Evetts is currently responsible for conservation at the Pierpont Morgan Library, New York. In common with many of her contemporaries she finds an ever-increasing knowledge of the book's structure and types of materials makes an invaluable contribution to her spare-time activity, creative binding. Her background is impressive – studying for three years under John Corderoy and John Plummer at Brighton College of Art, and three years under William Matthews at the Central School.

On completion of her training, she spent the summer of 1958 at the Roger Powell and Peter Waters bindery, and for the next nine years supported her binding activities with part-time lecturing (which included a four-year spell at Holloway Prison!). She was elected a Fellow of the Designer Bookbinders in 1965 and two years later went to the United States, where she taught full-time for a year in New York, then joined the Horton Bindery, and after a year moved to the Pierpont Morgan Library.

Her work illustrates a desire to complement not only the text but the typography – and since her design training was in this area, lettering in one form or another is often a feature of her covers. However, her approach is instinctive rather than calculated, because she has no specific philosophy about the role of the binder: 'To me it is such a natural process that if I like a book I am working on the ideas just flow.' If, for example, a book is profusely illustrated she tries to

come up with a design which is stylistically sympathetic to those illustrations; though never contrived.

Collections include: the Royal Library, The Hague, Holland; Johannesburg Public Library, South Africa; the Bodleian Library, Oxford; The Bridwell Library, Dallas, Texas; Humanities Research Center, University of Texas.

Donald Glaister, Palo Alto, California

Because there is no old-established tradition of fine binding in the United States, the really dedicated hand binders follow European influences. Don Glaister's first binding teacher, Barbara Hiller, had studied in Paris and, convinced of his enormous potential, persuaded him to go there, where he had private lessons in forwarding from Pierre Aufschnieder and in tooling from Roger Arnoult – to whom he gives much of the credit for his present style. 'He taught me to accept no compromise with myself,' Glaister recalls.

On his return to California in 1976, Glaister set up his own bindery, but felt his way with conventional bindings and repairs for local residents before taking the plunge with creative work. An early influence was Sam Richardson, a sculptor and professor at San Jose State University (where Glaister had gained a BA and MA in painting in art and sculpture):

He made sculptural landscapes out of plastic resins and painted them very subtly with lacquer. They were very soft and sensual to look at, never a straight line or flat plane. From him I learned to appreciate and love the softly undulating hills around San Francisco, and the lines their silhouette make. My work reflects his influence to this day.

I also learned from him that craftsmanship must be so good that it becomes invisible, that is, when the art is seen it is the *art* that is seen, and it is the *art* that provides the impact; not the way in which the materials are put together, no matter how expertly.

Although Glaister's style is very different from that of Ivor Robinson, he has a similar motivation; for instance he is inspired by handwriting and scribbling, which (in his case at least) he claims are one and the same thing. 'The ways people scribble and write with a pen are pure expressions, regardless of the words they may write. I use scribbles of my own as graphic devices to interpret particular texts, sometimes holding the pen and working with eyes closed.'

Jean de Gonet, Paris

Like Pierre Legrain, one of the binders he most admires, de Gonet has in less than ten years established *(right)* This binding of Vesalius' *De Humani Corporis* by Philip Smith is considered by Colin Franklin, a respected bookdealer and authority on fine bindings, to be one of the best of the twentieth century. In most of Smith's work, the designs on front and back covers are different, but in this massive tome on anatomy the skeleton figure in slight relief seems to be walking through the book. The back cover shows a rear view. The profile of a head is incorporated into the design. To give some idea of the complexity of the craftsmanship, the materials used are brown, tan and maroon oasis morocco, black elephant-hide inlay, maril and carved plastic onsets. Concealed behind the back square is a colourful image inset on a leather flyleaf.

(overleaf left) Although he had bound Tolkien's *Lord of the Rings* before, a commission in 1983 from an opthalmic surgeon in the United States, who wanted a binding that would stand in his surgery as an art-object, inspired Philip Smith to feature the searching eye of Sauron (the Lord of the Rings). Tolkien has described the eye in some detail – lidless but rimmed with fire, and having a baleful yellow iris with a black cat-like slit. Smith's client was able to contribute ideas based on his expert knowledge, and even sent an anatomical atlas of the eye, composed of sections through the eye printed on transparent leaves.

Smith had used cut-outs through the boards of bindings many years earlier, to combine an image with features seen through the 'windows'; he thought it would be appropriate to develop that idea in simulating the system used in the anatomical atlas, but doing so in an imaginative rather than scientifically exact way. So the book has the outer parts of the eye emerging from the cover of the book, with the iris built separately (from lightweight balsa wood covered with maril) on the flyleaf with a dark-blue suede surround. The slit through the iris reveals a darkness on the second flyleaf which is created by a painting of Sauron's dark stronghold. The back of the flyleaf pierced by the slit is treated to represent a kind of veining and optic nerve with fibrillated or branching red leather onlays. 'As the iris is textured with maril, I thought it would make it more meaningful by researching iridological markings,' Smith explains. 'Since the iris is divided into narrow zones representing parts of the body, blemishes and different textures in those zones depict illnesses, or the state of the various organs they represent. So one can read off

Sauron's characteristics from the positions of the various markings on the iris.' There are in fact *two* eyes, representing rival forces – the front cover being Evil, and the back, a landscape (ie opposing Sauron), Good. As the book is full of descriptions of mountain ranges, often impediments to the heroes' quest, Smith has stretched them along the rim of the covers. The curled ends of the eye are treated as handles for opening the book. When the book stands half-open, the volcanic landscape of Mordor may be seen in the doublure lining the back cover; this also sets off a mirror texture on the navy-blue suede flyleaf. The page edges are painted with relevant images.

(overleaf right) Behind the closed door of the mysterious room that is the outside design of Angela James' 1981 binding for *British Etchers 1850–1940* is an embroidered landscape, worked on silk, set into a thickness of board. The 'outside' of the room is covered in black and brown goatskin, the architrave of the door is wood under the goatskin, while the door itself is of millboard and card. Fittings – hinges, doorknob and nameplate – are of brass; the doublures are of green suede.

(overleaf right) Eleanore Ramsey has used the famous blackbirds baked in a pie on the cover of *Mother Goose*, a book of nursery rhymes. The birds are inlays of sterling silver. This is the first time she has worked in silver, apart from tooling. Here the tooling is palladium. The metals stand out vividly against the dark-blue French cape morocco.

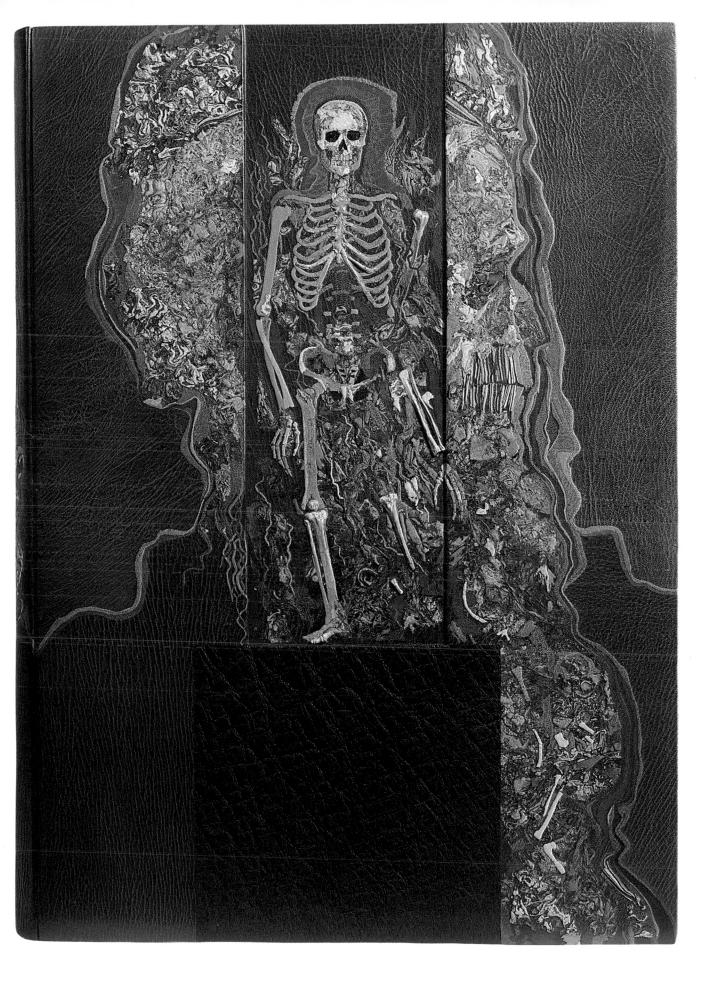

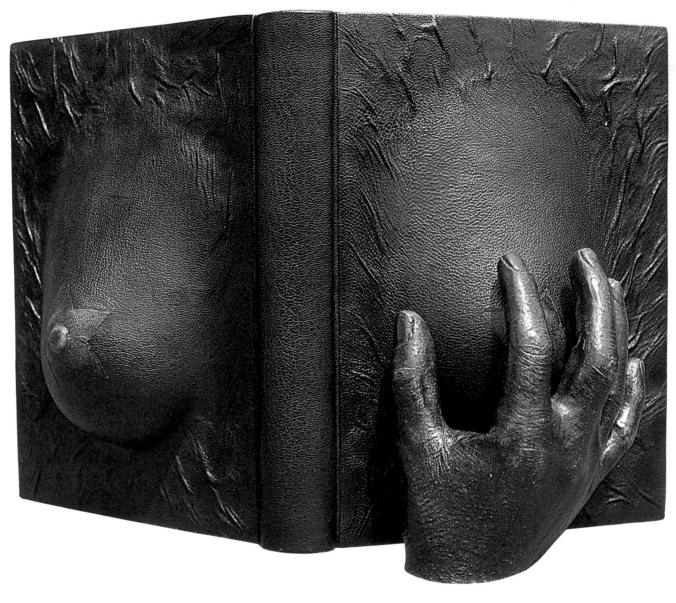

Gold tooling was all that Donald Glaister needed in this design for *Moby Dick*.

(*above left*) Dee Odell-Foster's binding for *The Visual Dictionary of Sex* was started when she was still a student at Camberwell. The breasts are formed from latex rubber (cast from a mould) under black leather, red-stained. The hand, cast from life, was originally painted plaster, but because of its fragility it was later cast in bronze.

(*left*) Dee Odell-Foster's *Motes*. The theme of social disintegration is expressed on 'boards' of black perspex to which oxidised metal is stuck. The relief is cast in silver plate. The 'flies' are soldered on, and the 'decay' symbolised by red resin seeping from the mass. The doublures are red suede. Having created the concept she commissioned Warren Stotely to write the text, which was then hand-printed.

himself as a craftsman of true originality. As discussed earlier, his style – although remarkably fresh – has a timeless quality about it, which makes him one of the few French binders whose work is not only in constant demand from collectors of modern bindings but who is also entrusted with the bindings of antiquarian and even medieval material.

De Gonet was virtually unaware of bookbinding until the subject was introduced at his college in 1967. He took an immediate interest but is largely self-taught, getting his professional training in the workshop of the Service de la Marine from 1971–5, when he started his own bindery. Working alone, he began in a conventional manner, but reacting against the 'jazzed-up' designs of so many French binders, gradually evolved his own philosophy. Rid of the convention of a decoration which he regards as merely grafted to the covers, he is left with an open choice at the start of each binding of the technique and materials to employ. Within the framework of his approach – to build on the basic structure of the book – these vary considerably.

One of the most remarkable features of de Gonet's work is the flexibility of the completed bindings. He can use even heavy and rigid materials, such as wood,

Conventionally concealed cords are not something associated with Jean de Gonet, but although his binding for *B*, by Pierre André Benoit, looks traditional enough, the materials are as unfamiliar as ever – the letter B inlaid in green box calf being carved from wood of the holly tree; the box is made from bark of the same tree.

and shape them into vertical slats to achieve uncharacteristic flexibility. This combination of precision craftsmanship with the naturalness of the leathers he prefers (complete with marks and flaws), adds a unique dimension to his work. Little of what he does with the spines, the cords and clasps – and even board-edges in a different material – can be taken simply at face value. They represent not only an inspired unity of form, but a conscious reluctance to disguise the execution of the binding – in other words, a rejection of arbitrary design.

De Gonet's talent was recognised from the start (he received his first commission in 1973), and through the lobbying of a group of astute booksellers and bibliophiles, the Bibliothèque Nationale in Paris staged his first exhibition in 1978. The promise has been maintained and, working full-time, his bindings to date total over 300.

Jiri Hadlač, Brno, Czechoslovakia

An artist of many talents – he is a painter, graphics artist and wood carver – Hadlač regards bookbinding as offering an opportunity of applying to a single work all the ideas and techniques that have interested him over the years. As indicated earlier, he experiments constantly, to the extent that on occasions he has produced miniature sculptures (eg a mechanical hunting dog from Ray Bradbury's *Fahrenheit 451*, and the transformation of Gregor Samsa into a beetle in Kafka's *Die Verwandlung*), which are impressive pieces of art, but have nothing to do with binding.

However, he is unquestionably a competent binder, having studied under one of the Czech master-craftsmen, Jindrich Svoboda, and his innovation — in structural terms — is confined mainly to decorating the covers. The most successful is his 'relief' technique of attaching to them pieces of leather and other small objects. The intention is not to illustrate or decorate, but to use the medium for expressing the essence of the story he has enjoyed (he seems to work exclusively on the work of authors he admires).

In his studio he has assembled, in addition to leather, a large variety of bizarre objects as parts of stuffed birds, plastic toys, artificial flowers, coins and spectacles — waiting to be used, some of them for years. From time to time he creates set-pieces from them, and the patterns originating in this way may become associated in his imagination with a book to be bound; an approach which is not so dissimilar to Ivor Robinson's scrapbook of sketches awaiting a binding.

It is likely that Hadlač's adventurous spirit will take him more and more towards the 'total book' concept, but meanwhile his present work is both interesting and challenging.

Collections include: Moravian Art Gallery, Brno.

The New Incas — containing 42 duotone screen-prints after photographs by Paul Yule — was the first book produced by Hadrill's New Pyramid Press, and was also bound by him (1983). Measuring 19 inches square, it was designed to look monumental and sculptural, reminiscent of the massive structures of the ancient Incas. The shapes on the front cover represent windows on the wall of a house in Cuzco, Peru. The doublures are of stone-coloured suede opposite grey Fabriano handmade endpapers.

Robert Hadrill, Rotherhithe, South London
There are a large number of young binders of promise; but very few are considered potentially outstanding while in their early twenties. However, such claims have been made on behalf of Robert Hadrill, who divides his time between creative binding, and running his own private press, the New Pyramid Press.

Hadrill is an instinctive craftsman; as a schoolboy he spent his spare time making things, anything from clay models and candles to jewellery and even notebooks and diaries. His first attempts at bookbinding were experiments on books borrowed from his father's collection — this before a two-year course at the Camberwell School of Art & Crafts. On leaving college he set up his own workshop, although he continued working one day a week for an experienced binder.

Since his first design binding in 1976, when he was interested more in the materials he might use to reflect the imagery of the book than in any artistic or literary influence, his approach has gradually changed, so that he is leaning more towards the total-book concept. Whether in his one-off bindings, or the limited-edition work of his private press, he has been motivated by the desire to project the book as a 'complete' object: no single element of the book should be dominant, or ignored, so that each part makes an equal contribution to the book's character, and the rhythm it emanates. However, he has found that rhythm increasingly difficult to achieve when re-covering a book that is already printed. Recently he has sought the responsibility for the content as well as the binding, preferring to work closely with a chosen author or artist.

It might be said that a craftsman needs the discipline of conventional commissions, binding a book with a completed content, but Hadrill is not the first to resist what he regards as a rein on his originality. During his active years, Edgar Mansfield accepted only one commission – and that was for a book he wanted to bind – because he felt that most interpretive designs were *simulations*, demanding skill but not true creativity.

Angela James, Northallerton, Yorkshire, England

One of the most visually entertaining stylists among the younger binders, Angela James was a winner of the Thomas Harrison Memorial competition early in her career, and a year later (1975) was elected a Fellow of the Designer Bookbinders. Bookbinding was merely a subsidiary subject when she got her Diploma in Printed Textiles from Glasgow School of Art in 1970, but it helped get her first job at the Cockerell Bindery, where she worked for two years under the unique guidance of Sydney Cockerell. In 1973 she helped set up the Eddington Bindery, staying until 1977 when she started her own workshop. She now operates, alone, full-time at binding – conservation as well as creative.

Taking her craftsmanship for granted, if asked to single out one highlight of James' style, most observers would suggest her flair for the best use of colour. She would concede that is the product of her training in textiles; indeed, the work of most fine binders reflects their early training or influences. She is a conventionalist in the sense that her designs are inspired by the theme of the book, which might at the same time also influence her choice of materials; the works of an Elizabethan poet, for example, could demand the use of velvet, in place of leather. However, she is a binder who takes the taste of her clients into consideration; she will suggest, but not impose.

Less interested in the philosophy of binding than many of her contemporaries, James allows her bindings to speak on her behalf; this seems to be successful, because there is an increasing interest in her work.

Collections include: the Lilly Library, University of Indiana and the University of Texas.

Trevor Jones, York, England

Sooner or later the careers of most artist-craftsmen arrive at a major crossroads, and the route they select may affect their lives dramatically. 1984 was such a year to the current Designer Bookbinders President, because it was the date he set himself to give up teaching and concentrate on creative binding. If the general acceptance of his work from collectors and fellow binders is anything to go by, he should do well. Some binders attract adulation from some quarters, and condemnation from others – but Jones' work is universally admired for the creative element, what he does with materials, and for his versatility.

After gaining a National Diploma in Design (Illustration) in 1953, he took a University of London Art Teacher's certificate the following year, while attending classes to learn bookbinding from Arthur Johnson who (with Bernard Middleton) was to form the Guild of Contemporary Bookbinders. Originally Trevor Jones took up binding because he considered it less competitive than many art disciplines, but he discovered he had an aptitude for it, and almost from the beginning his bindings were considered good enough to exhibit – very few of them failing to find a buyer. One of his exhibits so impressed the late Sir Basil Spence that he was asked to do the design for a Lectern Bible for the Chapel of Unity at Coventry Cathedral in 1962. But despite such interest, he was working full-time at teaching – and preferred not to accept commissions until more than ten years later, when after the British Bookbinding Today exhibition in 1975 the organisers, Kulgin Duval and Colin Hamilton, book-

An Intimate Landscape, by Leonard Clark, bound by Angela James in 1983, has a window (with wooden frame and 'glazed' with acetate sheet) cut through the front board, looking out on to a scene embroidered on silk set into the green suede flyleaf. The binding is in white calf, with wooden floor and skirting boards, complete with brass nails. Such perspective, especially in depth, is a feature of certain of Angela James's bindings; but in her 1982 binding, for a book of Edward Borein drawings by John Galvin (*below*), she achieves the same effect with onlay work at different levels. Borein's work deals mainly with the life and times of the cowboy, and Angela has captured the mood of the American mid-West by a design using leathers in terracotta, browns and yellow, highlighted with a couple of lines picked out in gold kid.

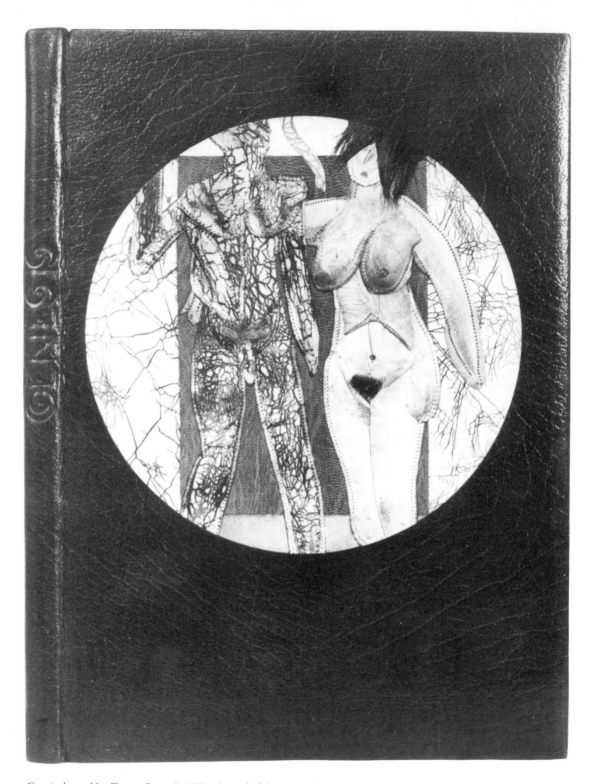

Genesis, bound by Trevor Jones in 1980, has a dark-brown Indian
buffalo calf skin, with the design in inlaid roundels of various
leathers (some dyed using flour-resist) and fur. The owner sent
Jones a photograph of Epstein's statue of Genesis, but her size here
results from a desire to make her more of an earth-mother than a
classical Venus, and the size of the finger-ends that emerged when
he unpicked the pair of old gloves he had used in constructing her
figure. The rear panel is of a group of the plants, birds and beasts of
Eden.

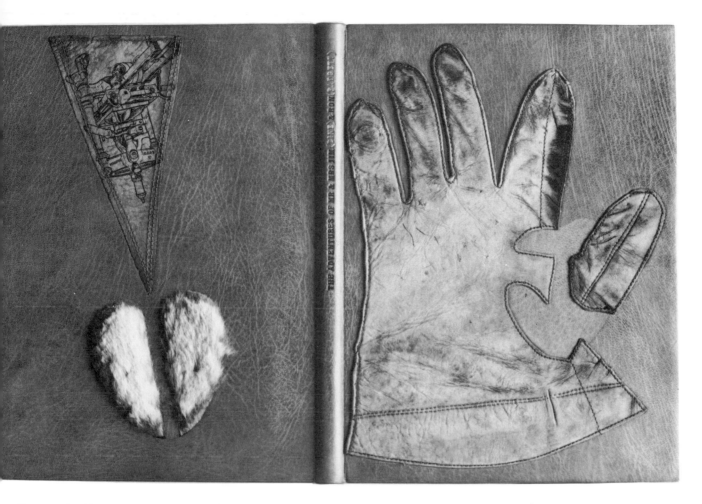

The spine text reads: THE ADVENTURES OF MR & MRS JIM & RON [PADGETT]

sellers and collectors, gave him the first of a series of regular commissions.

Jones' early influence was the bindings of George Fisher at the Gregynog Press, and the collection of twentieth-century French bindings in the Victoria & Albert Museum. From the design point of view those he admired were Paul Klee and the collagist Kurt Schwitters, and later Marcel Duchamp. His own etchings have been exhibited at the Royal Academy, but from the start he identified himself with fine binding. His light-hearted philosophy about binding may have had something to do with the fact that his work as a teacher-lecturer had taken care of the need to earn a living, so that his bindings had always been a 'self-motivated activity'; but it is unlikely that this will be affected by his change in status. The approach is not merely an attitude, but something he *feels*. 'Even when I'm binding a book for someone else I am, at the time of making it, making it for myself,' he says. 'In this way I feel I can indulge myself, let some humour into the binding – enjoy a freedom from the constraints of "good taste", and "proper respect for the text". I think delight, rather than reverence or awe, is the reaction to

Debris washed up on England's north-east coast is featured on the cover of this 1974 Trevor Jones binding for *Adventures of Mr & Mrs Jim & Ron*, a surreal type of book written by Ron Padgett and illustrated by Jim Dine, with hands and hearts a recurring theme. A major part of the design is a gauntlet work-glove, washed and cleansed of salt and unpicked, then stuck and sewn to the covering leather – an idea complete in his mind before he began work on the book.

be sought from those who see and handle modern bindings.'

Given more time in the future, Trevor Jones will accept many more commissions; there is, after all, the snag about bindings 'disappearing' at exhibitions. 'I feel very sad if one of my books is on show and someone buys it, and I've never met them, and I never see it again. I like to know clients. If I've had a client for some time then I enjoy the conversation with them about what they like, and what they would like in the future.'

Collections include: the British Library (including his first work, *Abu Roi*); the Victoria & Albert Museum; the Royal Library, Copenhagen; the Lilly Library, University of Indiana; University of Texas Library.

Daniel Knoderer, Valbonne, France

The most distinctive feature of Knoderer's art-deco style bindings is his rejection of the traditional rectangular boards in favour of softly curved shapes. Straight edges had become synonymous with binding, and while there was once a valid reason it no longer applies; so it is surprising that no one has emulated him. Curved edges in no way interfere with the book's function. But his standing sculptures are more controversial, although even the purists find it difficult to condemn Knoderer, because of his unquestioned skill as a craftsman.

The son of bookbinders, Daniel was dabbling in the craft even as a child. Apart from the thorough grounding obtained at home he was taught gold tooling by a specialist, Jules Fache, and during the ten-year period (1968–78) that he stopped binding, he was able to support himself as a gilder. But coupled with this instinctive skill is a restlessness that is only assuaged through constant experimentation. As remarked earlier, this urge for innovation has already achieved a number of breakthroughs. 'With each new work, it is essential to put everything back in the melting pot and start afresh. This provides stimulation for the mind, which in turn assists constant progress.'

Talking of the threat to the book from audio-visual systems and the like, Knoderer feels that we have to completely rethink our attitudes. 'The book is unique and we must stop thinking of the binding as utilitarian or as a decorative means of protection – but as a timeless work of art.'

In common with other creative binders, he is influenced by music, but to the extent that it is one of his main sources of inspiration and stimulation.

'Music is indissociable from my work,' he says. 'I play it and it is a vital part of my life. In my studio I often pass from bookbinding to music, to painting, to sculpture, to drawing, without any transitional phase. These means of expression carry the same vibrations. Listening to contemporary music provides a source of energy, sensation and meditation because its basic form is called into question. The creator absorbs, assimilates, analyses and puts his own interpretation on what he has heard.'

Jacqueline Liekens, Brussels, Belgium

One of the most distinguished artist-bookbinders in Belgium, Jacqueline Liekens' relatively short career to date is studded with honours and awards in recognition of her talent.

After a normal academic schooling, she studied bookbinding under Micheline de Bellefroid at the Institut National Supérieur des Arts Visuels in Brussels from 1966 to 1970. Two years later she was confident enough to begin working alone, and within another couple of years was given her first royal commission – a binding of *La Puissance et la Fragilité* for HM Queen Fabiola. The following year she won three silver medals in the Paul Bonet competition in Ascona, Switzerland, with *Un Rêve à Commettre*, by Patrick Waldberg. In 1977 HM King Baudouin of the Belgians asked her to bind Averaete's *Rubens et son Temps*, as a present for the King of Spain. In the same year he presented another of her bindings (*Joachim Lelewel*) to the President of Poland.

Jacqueline's prize winning continued with a silver medal at the Triennale Internationale de Reliure at Lausanne for Simone de Beauvoir's *La Femme Rompue*. Since 1981 she has supplemented her income by teaching part-time at the Brussels Institut des Arts et Métiers. Although her designs are usually presented in abstract forms, the inspiration for them generally comes from the content of the book (although not necessarily the title).

Bernard Chester Middleton, Clapham, London

Better known today for his work in conservation and restoration, and as an authority on the techniques of binding, Middleton still manages to produce two or three creative bindings every year, keeping above the minimum number required to retain his Fellowship of the Designer Bookbinders (he was President 1973–75 and he was of course founder-member of the Guild which preceded it). Bernard Middleton describes himself as a craftsman with no pretensions to talent as a designer; but he does himself an injustice. The many collectors who prize his bindings are concerned with the integrated whole, and not just because they are well made – something they can take for granted. If he is not able to rationalise his artistry, it may come from an innate aestheticism, never crystallised by a formal training in art, but which like a seam of gold waiting to be extracted from his subconscious gives him an instinctive feel for what is right. Not for nothing is he a Member of the Art Workers' Guild and Fellow of the Society of Antiquaries.

The son of a bookbinder who worked as a forwarder for Sangorski & Sutcliffe (on whose walls his name can still be seen among the list of distinguished apprentices later to make their mark), Bernard won a scholarship to Central School of Arts and Crafts, where his tutors included William Matthews. Following in the family tradition, he was apprenticed in 1940 to what was then the HMSO Bindery at the British Museum. The war had started, and just before joining the Royal Navy in

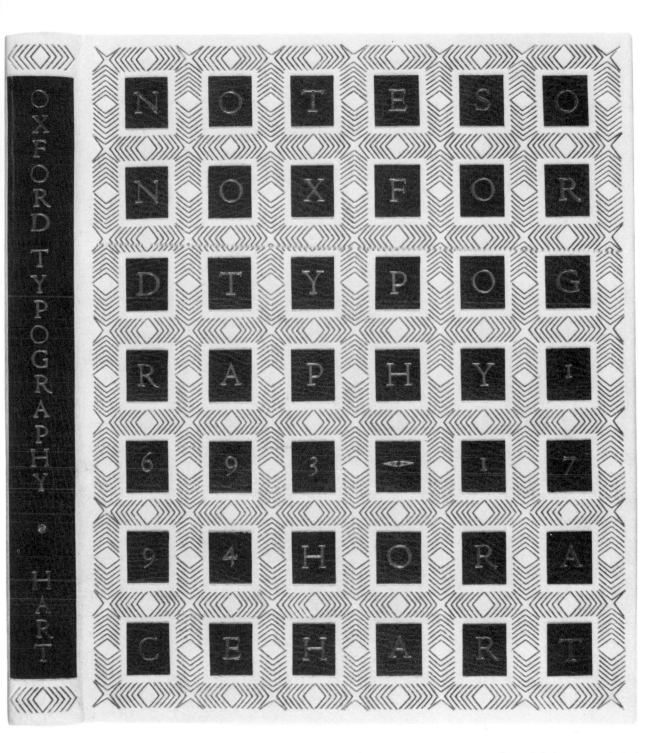

Behind what may appear a straightforward design, are technical problems only a binder would appreciate. *Notes on A Century of Typography at the University Press, Oxford 1693–1794*, by Horace Hart, was bound by Bernard Middleton in white tawed pigskin, and pigskin (because of its tautness) creates problems when trying to make gilt tooling stick. Each chevron is separately tooled, and he had to make three attempts, so the intricacy of the operation can be imagined. The onlays are in violet morocco, the doublures in violet suede.

1943, while still studying at evening classes he won a Silver Medal of the City & Guilds of London Institute for forwarding. Having returned to complete his apprenticeship, in 1949 he was appointed craftsman-demonstrator under Roger Powell at the Royal College of Art, where he stayed for two years. The following year he became manager of the Zaehnsdorf Bindery, but because of his consuming interest in restoration and conservation, he left to set up on his own.

Although he is first and foremost a binder, it is the *book* that Bernard Middleton loves, as his library of over 1,200 books and ephemera to do with production reveals. In 1983 the collection was acquired by the Rochester Institute of Technology, New York, for its College of Graphic Arts & Photography, on the understanding that much of it will remain in London as long as Middleton has professional need for it. On a recent visit I found one of his many fascinating assignments that have only a partial link with binding – a 1491 Old Testament Bible in Hebrew. The problem was to restore the book to its original state, but a major difficulty was that 119 sides were missing. £600 had already been spent on photographing the missing pages from another copy in the possession of the Bible Society. From the photos blocks would be made, while he found paper as near to the original as possible. He showed me the stock of old paper he has amassed for such purposes. Once assembled, it would be bound in period style complete with clasps. The job would be completed by repairing 'mistakes' made in a previous restoration in the nineteenth century when the paper edges were trimmed to precision sharpness; they would be sandpapered down to remove the sharpness of the corners.

He has written extensively, including: *A History of English Craft Bookbinding Technique*, 1963 and 1978 (Holland Press); and *The Restoration Of Leather Bindings*, 1972 and 1984 (American Library Association).

Collections include: the British Library; Victoria & Albert Museum; the Royal Library, The Hague, Holland; the Lilly Library, University of Indiana.

Dee Odell-Foster, Bradford-on-Avon, Wiltshire, England

Trained as a professional dancer, Dee Odell-Foster found expression for her creative urge in binding during a two-year course at Camberwell School of Art & Crafts. Although she only started producing bindings in 1980 she is considered one of the most original Fellows of the Designer Bookbinders. Odell-Foster's philosophy is interesting; while she is capable of designing a cover that stems directly from the author's theme, she will probably get more satisfaction from working on a book that has no text. In her view, the absence of words does not necessarily suggest absence of meaning, because the binding and content are interwoven and as the binder-creator, she is also the author:

The approach I have to my work is both complex and simple, definite and indefinite. It is a paradox that is hard to grasp at times, but I feel that for me the most important part of the work is the making of it. Everything is contained in the experience of the doing, and attaining perfection in the end result.

It is not enough for me every time to take a book and design an appropriate cover. The responsibility of the designer-binder is to put something of himself/herself into the design, and I find that the content of the book enforces certain constraints that impinge on the creative side of my work. While I recognise that elaboration and appropriateness are part of the creative function, I find that having the theme already defined by the content of a book stifles some originality.

Motes (illustrated) is an apt example – an exercise in which she created a binding on the theme of social decay, and then commissioned the content, thus reversing normal roles. Odell-Foster found the experience particularly stimulating and would argue that the resulting book is more 'hers' than the author's. She has, however, taken the idea to the next stage by binding two books without text at all.

Collections include: Humanities Research Center, Texas.

Eleanore E. Ramsey, San Francisco, California

The inspiration of this binder is the intrinsic 'beauty' of the book for what it is; completing it with a binding is a labour of love. She came to it by chance after graduating in academic subjects, and working in an antiquarian bookshop in Rockford, Illinois. It was there she discovered a catalogue of fine French bindings, the first beautiful hand bindings she had seen.

Getting little practical help from libraries, she took lessons from two binders in San Francisco, one being Barbara Hiller with whom she now shares some studio facilities (each of these having their own binderies). Workshops in specialised techniques followed, under the guidance of binders of the calibre of Christopher Clarkson (now with the Bodleian), Bernard Middleton, Philip Smith and Stella Patri. Her first work was exhibited in 1977 with the Hand Bookbinders of California.

Motivated by the conviction that the design of a book should be in harmony with the author's text, she is flexible in her approach, particularly with regard to materials, and her bindings have interestingly different features. She is, for example, keen on inlays, using metal and wood. Some of this means further specialist research and tests before she is able to achieve what she has in mind; time-consuming, but satisfying not only to those who appreciate her work, but especially to herself.

Constantly looking for new ideas, Eleanore Ramsey is currently working on a binding for Edgar Allen Poe's *Tales Of Mystery And Imagination*, featuring the front and rear of a coffin – which is not in itself especially novel. Her problem, requiring considerable research into metal behaviour, is finding a way to build-in concealed hinges that actually *creak* when the cover/coffin lid is opened!

Bruce Schnabel, Los Angeles, California

Although recognised for his talent as an individual, Bruce Schnabel does much of his work through the Artist's Book Consulting Service, which he set up in 1978 with the encouragement of Eudorah Moore, crafts co-ordinator of the National Endowment for the Arts, for the purpose of combining his energy and knowledge with artists who had not considered structure but were working in book format. The collaborative works mentioned earlier are the product of Schnabel's vision.

Schnabel began taking bookbinding classes while at the California College of Arts and Crafts, incorporating his art in book format. He was asked to take an apprenticeship and worked full-time to learn the craft for the next five years (with Ann Kahle, Capricornus School of Hand Bookbinding, California; Henry Brooks Ltd, in Britain; and H. Wayne Eley Associates, of New Haven, Connecticut). After that solid foundation he began doing restoration and conservation of rare books with period bindings. 'This gave me the opportunity to explore, art-historically, the evolution of book design since the first codices. I have applied this experience in my exploration of new design concepts.'

His first attempt to break away from conventional design bindings (at least, the 'abstract expressionistic interpretations of literature' that he deplores) was in 1976–7, when he created a group of fifteen journals without text to explore designs and use of materials – in this case derived from his interest in indigenous American fabric art (Southwest Indian blankets, Amish and other pieced quilts).

Collections include: Humanities Research Center, University of Texas; National Museum of Modern Art, Canberra, Australia; Metropolitan Museum, New York; Museum of Modern Art, New York; Chase Manhattan Bank, New York; Galerie Zabriskie, Paris; Galerie Jacques Fivel, Paris; Donglamur Foundation, Pennsylvania.

David Sellars, Holloway, North London

In common with other Fellows of the Designer Bookbinders, David Sellars does not have unlimited time in which to be creative – being obliged to teach for a living. Fortunately, he enjoys teaching and his tremendous energies and enthusiasms have inspired several talented binders who are more contemporaries than students. The point is made because Sellars' approach to binding makes it impossible for him to work quickly, and recognition of his qualities has been slower to arrive than for other book artists. Today, at thirty-five, he is at the threshold of a much wider acknowledgement of his true standing.

Sellars' early interest in art was broad. He studied part-time at Bradford College of Art and Leeds College of Technology while working as a printing apprentice. But the most significant impression was in 1972 when he saw two exhibitions in London on the same day – Barnett Newman at the Tate Gallery, and the Designer Bookbinders at the Victoria & Albert Museum. The first made him want to become an artist; the second provided him with a medium. 'It was the right choice. Today's painting is less exciting than crafts like bookbinding and pottery. I still do some drawing, but only towards the book as the end product.' His training consisted of a period at Camberwell School of Art & Crafts, and part-time at the Stanhope Institute, where he benefitted from the teaching skills and the dynamic ideas of Sally Lou Smith.

As explained earlier, David Sellars' books grow from an involvement with the text; it is central to his philosophy. Talking about writers to whose titles he has returned more than once – such as James Joyce – he says: 'My work on the book is intrinsic to what I see, so that the book becomes me. I've always done books because *I* want to . . . irrespective of whether they will sell . . . after all, it should be a really important event, and can take several hundred hours of my life.' For this reason he is wary of hand binders who can knock off a design, from conception to execution, within a matter of weeks.

Having said that he likes to establish a rapport with the author, Sellars does not make snap judgements, and will immerse himself in a text for months if necessary before he feels he is ready. 'I was once asked to bind a book of lectures by T. J. Cobden-Sanderson for a client in the United States. At first I thought we were so far apart in philosophical terms that I couldn't imagine doing it, but when I read the book and realised that what he was saying almost a century ago was still valid today, I was quickly on the same wavelength.'

For someone so bubbling with ideas, many very strongly felt, David Sellars is open-minded in his attitude to others. He is not an advocate, for example, of the French system – the division of responsibility. 'I cannot give up a part of the job – say the stitching – because the entire operation has to be mine. I have to be totally *involved* to make it work, and having two or three people involved can result in a lack of personality.' Nonetheless this does not stop him admiring a designer who cannot bind, and recognising his role in the craft.

Equally, for all his talk of 'involvement', he does not approve of the 'total book' concept, unless the artist is genuinely multi-talented.

I'm fascinated by Dante's *Divine Comedy*, for example, but Dante was a better writer than me, so I have to accept it. It's almost impossible to do everything properly. To make good art, one has to master the craft involved; you have to learn to mix paints so that they don't disintegrate. It is up to every artist – whatever the discipline – to get the craft right.

That is a statement which cannot be faulted, yet he is the first to admit that there can be exceptions who are multi-talented, one is a former pupil, Tim Ely.

Collections include: the British Library, and the University of North Carolina.

Faith Shannon, Ringmer, Sussex, England

Many of the binders featured in this book share a rich creative talent that is multi-faceted. Faith Shannon, for example, is an accomplished illustrator of books and advertising, as well as being one of the most interesting bookbinders. Throughout her career she has been singled out for awards and honours – the culmination of which was the MBE in 1977 for services to bookbinding; she is not the first but was certainly the youngest binder to be so honoured.

Like other potential painters, she came to bookbinding by accident – it was a required subsidiary subject at Belfast College of Art, and indeed she was taught by her painting tutor. Her general work was soon acquiring awards and prizes from Belfast and Dublin, but her interest in bookbinding remained mainly historical until she entered the Thomas Harrison Memorial Competition. Here her work was spotted by Edgar Mansfield, who encouraged her to use the various prize monies to pay for six months in London, at the Camberwell School of Art & Craft, and the London School of Printing, where he was one of the lecturers, and where she was the only girl among dozens of printing apprentices. Other teachers at that period were William Matthews, George Frewin and Hans Tisdall, but she also met others whose guidance was to prove invaluable, such as the artist Blair Hughes-Stanton.

From 1960 to 1963 she attended the Royal College of Art, in the Faculty of Graphic Design, but specialising in binding under Peter Waters. While there she was the beneficiary of an unusual bequest – some of the tools, and the press, used by Sybil Pye, and left to the Victoria & Albert Museum with the stipulation that what they did not need should be given to a 'promising student', preferably a girl, at the Royal College. She has them to this day. It was during this period that she utilised an earlier award from Dublin, the Henry Higgins Travelling Scholarship, to visit the United States.

In 1963 she began working for a living, remaining a freelance for seventeen years until she accepted the post of lecturer in charge of bookbinding at Brighton Polytechnic, which has meant a limit on the time she can devote to binding. As it happens, although she is capable of working and solving problems under pressure, Faith Shannon is reluctant to undertake more than half a dozen books a year, wary of jeopardising the freshness she can bring to each new binding.

The Designer Bookbinders vary in their attitude towards commissions; Shannon is one who prefers direct contact with a customer, which does not happen in the case of institutional bodies, or even booksellers. 'The inspirations come from the books, and in a way from the clients who commission. I always feel sad if a binding is bought by a dealer and I lose contact. I love to be there when I hand the book over. Even if the reaction is one of displeasure I'd prefer to know.' An interesting illustration of that point about feedback and the sense of co-operation is her 1977 binding in aluminium alloy of the Royal Institute of British Architects' Loyal Silver Jubilee address to HM The Queen – a commission she was not keen, initially, to accept. But having read an article on the uses of aluminium, she set out to learn about the subject and the enthusiasm generated all round made the binding design into something of a team effort, which gave her special satisfaction.

Collections include: British Library; Hornby Library, Liverpool; Lilly Library, Indiana; Crafts Council, London; Carlisle Museum, Cumbria; West Surrey College of Art, Farnham.

Sally Lou Smith, Kentish Town, London

One of the most admired of creative binders – she was

honorary treasurer of the Designer Bookbinders for six years, and President in 1979 – Sally Lou Smith has little time for the philosophical debate that continues to divide so many of her colleagues. She believes that the priorities of anyone prepared to devote their life to a craft that is inspired by a love for books and art should be to strive constantly for perfection in that work, and for greater unity among those who share that goal.

American born and educated, Sally Lou Smith came to binding relatively late, and more from curiosity born of her love of books, than to fulfil a long-term ambition. Having married a fellow-American and settled in Paris, she found a home-from-home in her father-in-law's large personal library, which apart from its literary appeal whet her appetite for knowledge about the book as an object. When her marriage ended,

The poems in *Names of the Lost* by Philip Levine are full of detail – a build-up of remembered fragments – and Sally Lou Smith's binding in 1983 has a beautifully haunting quality. The coloured goatskins are inlaid on the black, with crumpled goatskin (black and grey) onlaid.

she intended to return to the United States but first came to England for a holiday – and stayed. That was in 1958, and she was fortunate enough to come under the enthusiastic guidance of John Corderoy at Camberwell School of Art, where she remained for four years.

Sally Lou Smith had come from a 'do-it-yourself' family, and was not unfamiliar with tools, but in bookbinding she found her forte. A full-time student, she was sufficiently inspired to continue working on her own after classes, even through the holiday breaks in the course. It is this obsession with books (she does

121

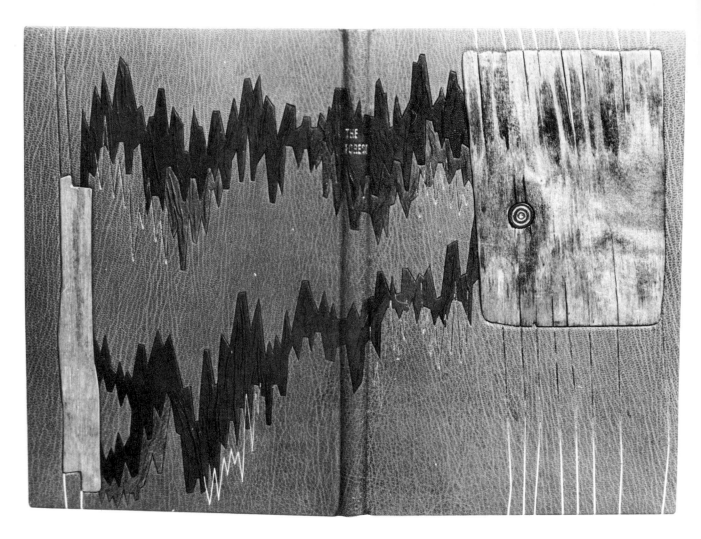

To use wood in a binding (1979) of *The Forest*, by Janet Rodney and Nathaniel Tarn, seemed natural. Sally Lou Smith covered the boards in beige goatskin, with two thin panels of weathered wood semi-recessed, and with grey and tan crumpled-goatskin onlays. The strong markings in the wood are extended in both colour and pattern in leather, and the cracks tooled in gold.

not set out to collect, but like so many compulsive bibliophiles, somehow manages to attract books like a magnet) that makes her reluctant to provide her bindings with a box, because she feels that the book should be exposed and immediately accessible.

Such dedication – coupled to an instinctive talent for design – could not go unrewarded. The first of her prizes was in the Thomas Harrison Memorial Competition in 1961, and she was a winner again in the following year, and the next. As a professional she gained first prize in Major Abbey's Bookbinding Competition in 1965, was honoured with a 'one-man' exhibition at the Galleria del Bel Libro, Ascona, Switzerland, in 1974 (only the third 'British' binder to be so honoured), and three years later received the

British Craft Award for bookbinding. From the very beginning her work was in demand, and the Victoria & Albert Museum in 1962 was the first of her customers, for a design binding of *England's Helicon*, a remarkable achievement for someone at the very start of her career.

She supplements her income from teaching, but her output over the years has not only been prolific, but fascinatingly different. People having seen her work at museums or at exhibitions, and perhaps familiar with only one of her phases, offer enthusiastic but contradictory advice, such as 'Her strength is her gold tooling', or 'She can't be equalled at manipulating leather'. In fact many of these claims are justified. Like any artist of ideas she has a low threshold of boredom, and is constantly trying new techniques to create different effects. 'A binder needs to experiment. A technique occurs to me and I might play around with it for several years until something clicks. Mind you, with leather, a lot can happen by accident. The first time I used puckering in a design, it was by accident.'

For the same reason there is no apparent long-lasting

122

pattern to her work; her gold tooling is superb, for instance, but she does not use that as excuse for employing it all the time. 'Each book is different and has its own problems – functionally, as well as in design and structure.' Talking of gold, she adds: 'I love it. Not only is it effective, but in the course of time when all the leathers have turned to various shades of murky brown, gold-tooled bindings will still be glowing from library bookshelves. But as much as I admire its vitality, it is sometimes too elegant for the design ideas I want to develop.'

Collections include: British Library; Victoria & Albert Museum; Spencer Collection of the New York Public Library; Birmingham Reference Library; Lilly Library, Indiana; Rosenback Foundation, Philadelphia.

Jan Sobota, Liestal, Switzerland

Czech craftsmanship is associated most with handmade glass, but it has a fine tradition in bookbinding, and it is a tragic reflection on the current political system that the brilliant Jan Sobota was obliged to leave the country in 1982 and seek political asylum in Switzerland (although he may eventually settle in the United States). His voluntary exile followed continued harassment from the authorities when he refused to stop contact and correspondence with fellow binders in Western Europe.

Sobota is best known today for the exciting freshness of the ideas he incorporates into his bindings and book objects, but his career began conventionally as an apprentice to master-binder Karel Silinger. While at the studio he became friendly with Josef Hodek and Jan Wenig, who were to influence his conception of artistic binding. He also commuted to Prague to attend the School of Applied Arts, from which he graduated in 1957. After working for another master-bookbinder and for one of the State Co-operatives in 1962, he was appointed Head of the Bookbinding department of the 'Spring' Co-operative in Carlsbad, where he supervised eleven craftsmen in all the bookbinding disciplines, but including graphics, lithography, woodcuts and

Sally Lou Smith's 1982 binding of Gogol's The Overcoat *has some subtle as well as obvious associations with the subject of the book. Although tan goatskin forms the basis of the covering, a mesh pattern blocked into the leather hints at the shape of the overcoat, while the hemp stitching on the inlaid black goatskin, and strips of frayed unbleached linen, suggest tailor's materials.*

(above) One of Jan Sobota's infrequent illustrative designs – for Daphne du Maurier's *The Birds*.

(above right) Sally Lou Smith's 1983 binding for *The Engravings of David Jones* features a complex conception designed to look simple. Covered in dark-brown cape morocco with crumpled dark-green onlay. Cut-outs reveal two panels of wavy-striped goatskin onlays, in shades of beige, green and grey, with blind tooling. The stripes evolved from an initial thought suggesting wood engraving; the tree shapes derive from David Jones's frequent use of them.

(right) Sally Lou Smith used colour as an unusual form of symbolism in her 1982 binding of Joyce's *Ulysses*. Colours indicate the progression of day, dawn to dark; slate and sandpaper show Dublin; gold rectangles are the lighted windows of the city; blind lines are wanderings. Note the recessed sandpaper panel mounted with fragments of slate.

(overleaf) The blaze of colour from delicate onlays on navy-blue morocco does not lessen the impact of gold tooling in this 1981 binding by Deborah Evetts of *Ourika*, written by Claire de Durfort, translated by John Fowles.

124

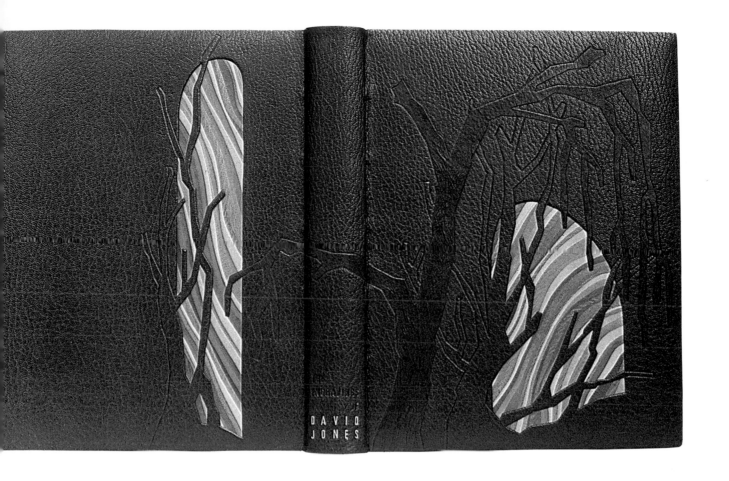

THE ENGRAVINGS
OF
DAVID
JONES

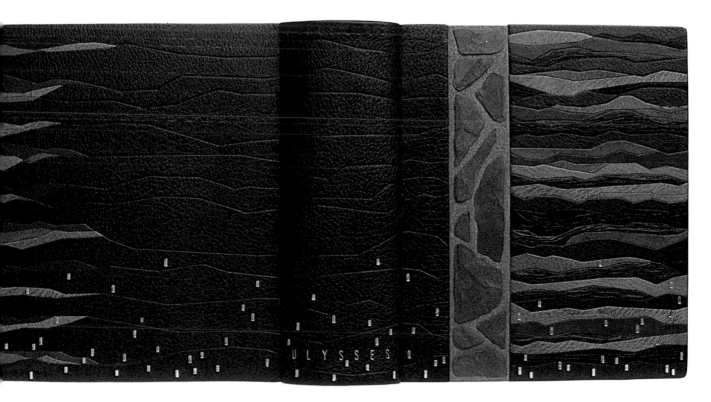

ULYSSES

(above left) Jeff Clements' binding in 1980 for *The Vision of William Concerning Piers the Plowman* was his third for this title – the others were in 1967 and 1973. It superbly illustrates his interest in landscape as a theme.

(left) This binding by Bryan Maggs of *Seven Pillars of Wisdom* is my favourite of the eighteen bindings of this title in the collection of Colonel Bradfer-Lawrence. Bryan Maggs is a partner in Maggs Bros, the old-established London antiquarian booksellers, and is a leading authority on the history of English binding. Almost dismissing himself as 'only a part-timer', Maggs's output is regrettably limited by his other interests. In fact he was trained by William Matthews and is a Fellow of the Designer Bookbinders.

(above) This Sobota binding (1967) of Kipling's *The Jungle Book* features snakeskin, with calf.

engraving – inevitably doing most of the skilfully demanding jobs himself. During this nine-year period he profited artistically from close collaboration with the graphic artist V. Hakl.

In 1971 Sobota set up his own studio in Carlsbad where, in addition to fine binding, he carried out restoration work and the production of facsimiles of old bibles and psalm books. The restoration work included one mind-boggling order from the town of Jachymov, which had a Latin library of 236 rare volumes – the oldest printed in Germany in 1475 and the latest, from Basle, 1629. He also filled orders for artistic leatherwork as decoration. Leaving Czechoslovakia without his tools, he was obliged to set up his new bindery with a nucleus of new self-made tools and contributions from binders from other countries. Now, having acquired a number of steady customers from museums, libraries and private collectors, he supplements his income by demonstrating bookbinding techniques part-time at the Paper Museum in Basle.

In 1969, before his work began to attract international attention (bringing him into contact for the first time with the secret police), he was presented by the Czech Minister for Culture with the title 'Master of Applied Arts in the Field of Bookbinding', making him only the twelfth bookbinder accorded that honour. The following year in Carlsbad he was given his first one-man exhibition. Nine others were to follow, and he has taken part in eleven collective exhibitions in Czechoslovakia and four in other countries. As a result he was admitted to the German MDE (International Association of Artistic Bookbinders) in 1977, and he joined Designer Bookbinders two years later.

Jan Vrtílek, Žilina, Czechoslovakia
Every creative binder is influenced, even subconsciously, by the work of others, but Jan Vrtílek, born in 1906, and the man who has set the pace in modern Czech binding, had little opportunity to compare notes, and had to find his own way. During World War II, under the German occupation, his contact with other Czech artists and binders was severely restricted, yet by the 1950s his work was already on a par with the best emerging from Western Europe. His 1963 binding for Oszka Bethlen's *Život v říši smrti (Life in The Realm of Death)*, using old, torn dog-skin, decorated with mosaic and braille lettering, is surely one of the outstanding bindings of the decade. His work has remained as fresh and inventive as that of binders half his age or less.

Vrtílek was apprenticed to a leather binder in Moravia, and when twenty-one was employed by the well-established Ludvik Schönpflug bindery at Brno. His exceptional talent was already evident, and the following year (1928) some of his bindings were shown at the major Exhibition of Contemporary Culture held at Brno. It was from this platform that he moved to Žilina and set up on his own, although for the next ten years he struggled to make a living, and his creative work was limited. After the war, renewed contact with Czech artists recharged his creative batteries and a friendship with the respected binder Jindřich Svoboda helped him achieve that elusive unity of art and craft. In 1958 he won first prize at the Third All-Slovak Exhibition of Applied Art.

In 1982 he contributed to his fiftieth exhibition (five of them devoted to him alone) and many were held abroad, in Budapest, Bucharest, Berlin, Leipzig, London, Cairo, Munich, Montreal and Vienna. When people talk of a national 'style' it has been said that many of Vrtílek's bindings could only have been created in Slovakia – and only by him.

Vrtílek has always enjoyed gold tooling, a feature of his 1970 binding of *Vitava*, by K. Plicka. It is on a green background, the onlay being in grey.

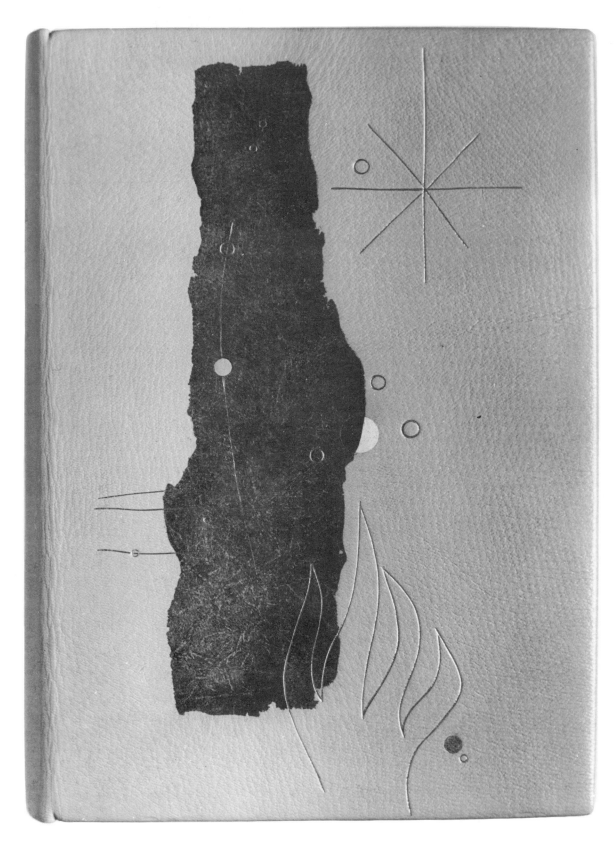

Vrtílek's 1966 binding of Dante's *The Divine Comedy*; onlay in light
ochre and relief design in gilt.

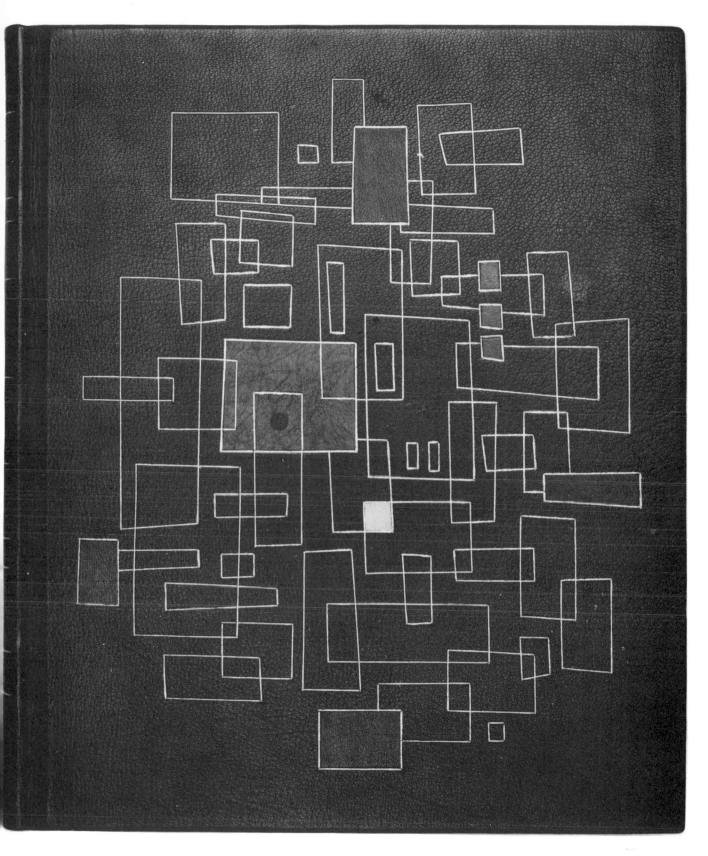

Striking use of coloured inlays as part of a mosaic pattern in the
1965 binding by Vrtílek of Karol Kelley's *Italy Today*.

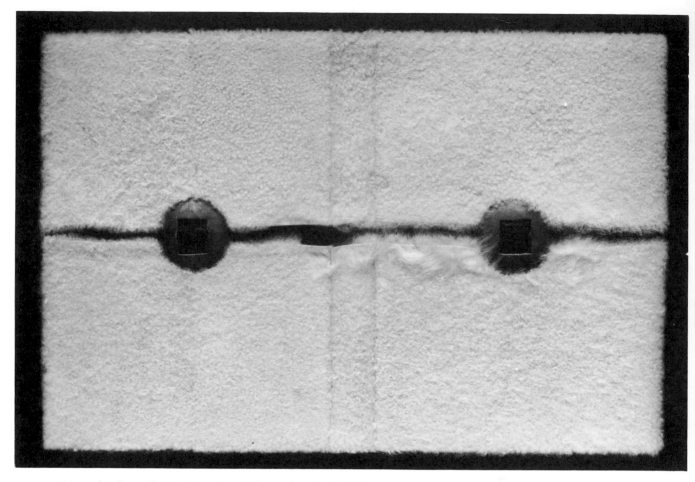

Recent bindings of Vrtílek's, such as this one done in 1979 for *Slovak Folk Tales*, feature other materials. Here brass buckles are inlaid on green leather reversed, which contrasts stongly with the pale lambskin.

One of the most adventurous of German binders is Peter Weiersmuller. This 1979 binding of Erica Jong's *Angst Vorm Fleigen (Fear of Flying)* is an ingenious mixture of wood, leather, painted paper and collage. The 'wings' flap on small springs. The pop-up photograph is of the author.

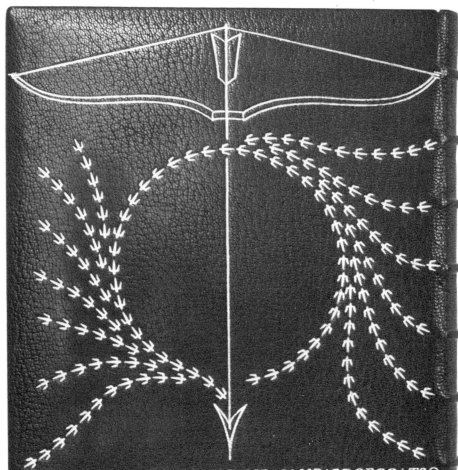

THEOVERTHROWNHERAISDANDASAHEARDOFGOATSO
RTIMEROUSFLOCKTOGETHERTHRONGDDROVETHEM
BEFOREHIMTHUNDER-STRUCKPURSUDWITHTERROR
SANDWITHFURIESTOTHEBOUNDSANDCHRYSTALLW
ALLOFHEAVNWHICHOPNINGWIDEROWLDINWARDAN
DASPACIOUSGAPDISCLOSDINTOTHEWASTFULDEEPT
HEMONSTROUSSIGHTSTROOKTHEMWITHHORRORB
ACKWARDBUTFARWORSEURGDTHEMBEHINDHEADLO
NGTHEMSELVSTHEYTHREWDOWNFROMTHEVERGEO
FHEAVNETERNALWRAUTHBURNTAFTERTHEMTOTHE
BOTTOMLESSPITHELLHEARDTHUNSUFFERABLENOISE
HELLSAWHEAVNRUININGFROMHEAVNANDWOULDHA
VEFLEDAFFRIGHTEDBUTSTRICTFATEHADCASTTOODE
EPHERDARKFOUNDATIONSANDTOOFASTHADBOUND

Roger Powell's 1975 binding for a Nonesuch Press edition of
Milton and Blake, featuring characteristic lettering.

136

8

COLLECTING BINDINGS – FINE, FANCIFUL AND FREAKISH

At the outset, I settled for compromise in using 'fine' binding as an umbrella term for binding of the highest quality in art or craftsmanship. Yet just as bibliophiles will collect material that is offbeat – doing so for a variety of reasons that have no bearing on such normal considerations as literary merit – so some collectors of bindings are at times tempted to ignore quality in favour of novelty.

Under the broad heading of 'art' there have been a number of attempts to feature books and bindings in settings that deliberately deny their basic function, to be opened and read. It is twenty-five years since the Tate Gallery in London presented the works of an 'artist' who stuck books, edges out, on a plaster canvas – 'treating' them first with a blowtorch. More recently

two New York artists have featured 'sealed' books in their works – Stella Waitzkin, feeling that civilised society suffers from a surfeit of words, created solid 'books' from plaster and resin, and even a *Memorial Library*, which consisted of shelves full of 'dead' books. Using similar techniques, Barton Benes has built a 'book' on wheels, entitled *Travel Book*, and another called *Bound Book*, which is a token volume symbolically encased in rope and decorated in boot polish.

Only slightly less offensive to bibliophiles is the *Untouchable Book* made in 1974 by Lucas Samaras, and featuring knives, pins and razor blades (illustrated). At least, here the point is made without destroying the

The *Untouchable Book* produced by Lucas Samaras in 1979.

book by glueing the pages together; given the will, we can still (theoretically) get at the text!

But such works are more at home in an art gallery, and those interested in them are art collectors; whereas, in the main, bindings – no matter how arts-orientated – are sought by book collectors. Indeed, with the exception of books with a dual appeal, such as the works of Bruce Schnabel and Tim Ely, the patrons of fine binding are overwhelmingly booksellers and bibliophiles. Even they are not immune to gimmickry.

Some years ago I saw a most unusual collection of bindings in an antiquarian bookshop in Manhattan. The books had belonged to Maurice Hammoneau, a French antiquary, who recased each volume in a binding appropriate to its subject; since most concerned animals, wild and domestic, the visual effect of a couple of rows on the bookshelf can be imagined. Hammoneau's peculiar hobby began when he bought a book on the Foreign Legion called *Greater Love Hath No Man*, by Alice Weekes (Boston, 1939). Since he had flown in the distinguished Lafayette Escadrille squadron in World War I and was fascinated by military tradition, he rebound the book in the dark and light-blue uniform of a legionnaire, with gilt buttons on the spine, campaign ribbons and *fourragères* mounted on the cover. As though to prove it was tradition, and not patriotic fervour, that had inspired him, he bound a copy of Erich Maria Remarque's *All Quiet on the Western Front* in the rough field-grey cloth uniform and brass buttons of the German infantryman of that era, less ornate and sombre enough to match the literary content. Subsequently, Hammoneau developed a passion for big-game hunting, and started binding appropriate titles in skins of the animals and reptiles he killed, skinning and tanning these himself. The list is unusual enough to reprint:

Ostriches and Ostrich Farming, London, 1879
8vo, bound in ostrich hide with a gilt onlay ostrich decoration, with special handmade ostrich-decorated silk endpapers.

Pig-Sticking, or Hog-Hunting, London, 1889
8vo, wild boar hide, pictorial gilt onlay of boar-hunting scene, specially made silk endleaves.

The Water Buffalo, Saco, Maine, 1922
4to, buffalo hide, specially made silk endpapers.

Modern Milk Goats, Philadelphia, 1921
8vo, full morocco, specially made decorated silk endpapers.

The Individuality of the Pig, New York, 1928
8vo, full pigskin.

A Voyage to the Arctic in the Whaler Aurora, Boston, 1911
8vo, full black sealskin, spine lettering inlaid in white sealskin, seal portrait onlaid in seal fur on the cover, specially made decorated silk endpapers, slipcased.

Shark! Shark! New York, 1934
8vo, full sharkskin, specially made decorated endpapers.

Reptiles of the World, New York, 1933
8vo, full python, specially made decorated silk endpapers.

The History and Romance of the Horse, New York, 1941
8vo, full cordovan.

The American Shepherd, New York, 1845
8vo, full vellum, gilt decorated leather labels, specially made decorated silk endpapers.

The Alligator and its Allies, New York, 1915
8vo, full alligator, marbled endpapers.

Dragon Lizards of Komodo, New York, 1927
8vo, full lizard, specially made decorated silk endpapers.

Marsupials, London, no date
8vo, full kangaroo, gilt decorated, silk endpapers.

Cutaneous Diseases, Philadelphia, 1818
8vo, full human skin.

With a Camera in Tigerland, New York, 1928
4to, full untanned tiger fur. Specially made decorated silk endpapers.

Lion, New York, 1929
4to, full untanned lion fur, hand-painted grass-cloth endleaves.

Our Reptiles and Batrachians, London, 1893
12mo, cloth, ten colour plates, with *Snakes*.

Snakes, London, 1882
8vo, cloth. Enclosed in a compartmented book box, of full boa, with *Our Reptiles and Batrachians*.

Wild African Animals I have Known, by Prince William of Sweden, London, 1923
4to, full Grévy's zebra, untanned, the mane forming the back-strip, specially decorated silk endpapers.

The Seal Islands of Alaska, Washington, 1881
4to, full seal, silver decorated with silver-tooled ornaments on covers, specially made decorated silk endleaf.

The asking price for the collection in 1977 was $5,000 and interest in such bizarre material must be limited, yet a few years later I discovered that the collection had been sold.

At a time when there is a debate about how far a binding can depart from the traditional form to stand as a piece of art or sculpture in its own right, there is (coincidentally) some speculation over the 'folly' of putting a fine binding on a relatively worthless book: a book, it is said, has to be worthy (in terms of literary or rarity value) if it is to justify the attention of a collector. The book-or-the-binding argument reminds me of an interesting analogy, when a silver *objet d'art* turned up at Hodgson's Saleroom in London in the mid-1970s. The silver specialists, recognising a seventeenth-century example of early miniature silverware, considered it might be worth about £200. However, almost as an afterthought it was passed to the book department, where it was eventually identified as the only known copy of a 4½in primer by John Owen, Welsh minister and theological writer of the 1650s – initially disguised by its contemporary silver binding. Auctioned as a book, it fetched £700.

The inevitable conclusion is that the bibliophile will pay for the binding of a book in which he or she has a special interest. In time this may change, but until the artist-craftsman can identify new and potential markets, he or she can be in uncharted waters where there are no established guidelines. One of the talented American binders mentioned in this book provides an interesting comparison. 'The old Mercedes Benz limousines are exceptionally popular here, and I think it is probably easier to get $1,000 for the re-upholstering of one of these in imitation leather, than to get $1,000 for a well made and handsomely designed binding.'

In many ways the history of design binding, which could not have survived without people to buy, did not begin until the formation of the Guild of Contemporary Bookbinders in 1955, because it was only then that the first exhibition to a wider audience was held – at the Foyles Gallery in London. Indeed, the Guild's few members were hard put to produce enough material for display. Edgar Mansfield remembers it as the most significant development of the decade, vividly recalling the two most important collectors of the time – Major Abbey and Albert Ehrman – arriving on the dot of opening time. 'They raced round, almost competing with each other to buy,' he says. What he did not know was that they were not quite the first – Christina Foyle would slip in before the doors opened to earmark anything that *she* particularly liked!

The Foyles exhibition was held annually, and rapidly grew in status. The next important collector to take an interest in modern bindings was Maurice Goldman, who was so fascinated that he immediately commissioned bindings from Ivor Robinson and Edgar Mansfield – the first Mansfield had accepted (in fact, the only one, apart from the New Zealand Government's wedding present to Princess Anne some years later). However, he is quick to point out it was not so much the commission that he accepted, but an opportunity to bind a particular book, *Gargantua*. To Mansfield, who had no problems selling most of the work he produced to satisfy himself, there should be no 'conditions' tied to an artist's freedom of expression; a commission represents compromise, and the 'winning' of a competitive activity – whereas the truly creative act is simply a compulsion from within.

The name Foyles has become synonymous with size, and few people realise that it actively sponsors and patronises not only bookbinding, but paintings, the fine arts, embroidery and even jewellery design. 'Our gallery is lent freely to artists and craftsmen because I am so very interested in anything beautiful,' concedes Christina Foyle, 'and institutional bodies like the British Museum come to buy.' Because of her own regard for books, she has collected fine bindings from the early days. 'Most of the material I have bought over the years has quadrupled in value, but my reason for the purchase was for their beauty, not investment, and to encourage the artists – which we shall go on doing as long as we are around.'

It is scarcely surprising that some of the most enthusiastic collectors and patrons of fine bindings are antiquarian booksellers, since they have to be lovers of books to become involved in the first place. Two of the most influential in recent years have been Kulgin Duval and Colin Hamilton, of Pitlochry, Scotland, and Colin Franklin, of Oxford, England. The influence of the former has been most widely noticed through the major exhibitions they have mounted. Within a couple of years of their initial interest, in 1975, a collection of forty bindings, British Bookbinding Today, was shown, representing some of the best work currently available from British binders. The collection was sold *en bloc* to the Lilly Library, Indiana. Subsequently the partners commissioned thirty bindings from Sydney Cockerell – whose work (with Joan Rix Tebbutt) they consider exceptional – most of which sold from their catalogue (1980), although significantly some were kept back for their own collection. The bindings were also exhibited at the Fitzwilliam Museum, Cambridge.

Cockerell provides a clue to Duval and Hamilton's personal taste, which is in the mainstream of design binding, although one of the binders they most admire is Trevor Jones, very much an innovator. Indeed their interest is wide ranging. They are not enthusiastic, perhaps, about the concept of the binding as an art object, and are less interested in a craftsman's philosophy or approach than the work itself.

Colin Franklin, coming to bookselling after twenty years in publishing, having made his mark there as managing director of one of Britain's best-known firms, maintains a lower profile in keeping with his unusual bookselling philosophy. Franklin is motivated by his love of books to concentrate on buying only books that he likes and would like to possess – so that they can in turn be passed on for the enjoyment of others. By dealing in fewer and fewer books, as opposed to collections, or even replenishing stock (a major headache for most people in the trade), he remains unique among antiquarian booksellers; and because he is prepared to buy for himself he has been a patron of the book arts. Philip Smith was talking of giving up full-time binding, during a low ebb in his career, when Franklin stepped in to buy his 'book walls'.

An authority on all matters relating to the history of books, writers and artists, his catalogues have been works of scholarship, and he is the author of *Private Presses* (London, 1969). It is this awareness and appreciation of what has gone before that makes his own attitude especially interesting. In a paper – appropriately entitled 'Binding: In Defence of Decadence' – presented to the Humanities Research Center, Texas, he talked of the 'religion' of books, espoused by Cobden-Sanderson, but continuing:

Something or someone, book or collector, would appear to have gone off course; the two opposing views of a book, coveted treasure or functional text, are following collision courses. One opened it reverently, barely touching the leaves, another flung it upon the table or shoved it in his pocket while he stared in speculation at the stars. For one binding became art, which the other destroyed. I believe now that with bindings we should emphasise the history of books rather than their art. Bless them if they rise towards art, that's a bonus, but view them rather as touching evidence of 'this man's art and that man's scope'.

An argument for tolerance, perhaps, yet more than that because Franklin's buying pattern is, by his own admission, irrational. He buys a limited number of design bindings because of their individual appeal – yet is just as happy with a fine manuscript, or example of fine printing, housed in an ordinary box. He does not approve or disapprove of fringe art forms, or the different philosophies of binding as an art; it is always the object itself that matters.

Among the collectors who have no interest in resale values is Colonel Philip Bradfer-Lawrence. His hobby, inspired by his father's bibliophilic interests, began in 1938 with the desire to collect anything by or about Colonel T. E. Lawrence (no relation). His fondness for bookbinding developed from an early ambition to produce fine books such as those turned out by the Ashendene Press by St John Hornby, but he soon realised that printing of that quality required substantial capital, while very good binding could be done with the minimum of equipment.

After World War II, still in Austria with the British Army, he began to take private lessons – only to give up almost twenty years later when he bought a controlling interest in Zaehnsdorf, and realised how 'amateur' (his words) were his own efforts. Although there are important bindings in his collection, by an interesting selection of binders, the nucleus is built around Lawrence's *Seven Pillars of Wisdom* – to date he has eighteen copies of this one title, by different binders.

An outsider might regard collectors like Bradfer-Lawrence as the 'patrons' of today because any craftsman surely needs such support. Yet his experience in finding many of them almost diffident in fulfilling orders is not untypical. He has frequently been kept waiting for commissions to be completed – the record being four years and one month; another binder took over three years even to acknowledge receipt of the book that had been sent for binding. Practically all in the *Seven Pillars* series were commissioned, along with a box or slipcase, but Edgar Mansfield's binding was obtained from a London firm of booksellers; it had no protection, so Bradfer-Lawrence was able to call on his own neglected binding skills to make a sand-coloured fall-back book box, lined with salmon-pink artificial suede. Despite his misgivings it looks very professional.

Although John Keatley is a bibliophile, his collecting interests extend to a range of twentieth-century arts and crafts. Some years ago he set himself the target of compiling a record of what (in his opinion) is best in British painting, sculpture, glass, china and, of course, books. These collections, through the Keatley Trust, will be bequeathed to the nation.

Mr Keatley's decision to limit his acquisitions to items produced by British artists and craftsmen is more responsible than might be imagined, because like any collector of sensitivity he is the first to acknowledge the fact that British work in these areas is not always the best. But for obvious reasons there had to be parameters, and he has tried to ensure that his judgements in these relatively narrower categories will still be valid long after his death.

Most of his bindings have been commissioned.

Through studying the work of binders he admires, and knowing the books he wants bound, that is the author and illustrator as well as the book, he has an intuitive feeling about the sort of book that is going to bring out the best in a binder. In the past eight years he has secured thirty in this way from among the leading binders, and almost all were successes. On the other hand he is constantly on the lookout for earlier material, and only recently Philip Smith's magnificent *Vesalius* was added to the Keatley Trust collection.

As a connoisseur of art, Mr Keatley does not much care about binders' philosophies. He makes no distinction between art and craft; bindings, like pictures are either 'good' or 'bad'. Maintaining that 'Books are for reading; bindings are for protection; decoration is for delight', he nevertheless keeps an open mind about the approach or the quality of any work until he has seen it. 'What really matters,' he says, 'is what people are going to think of them in a hundred years' time.'

The failure in recent years of successive British Governments to support the arts which need subsidies has meant that institutions never have sufficient funds to obtain the material they need. The Bodleian Library, part of the University of Oxford but second only to the British Library in size and status, depends almost entirely on the sympathetic support of friends. The British Library is in an unenviable position, having to divide its limited resources to meet a variety of demands that never diminish; indeed, with the passage of time, can only increase. The enormous financial strain of conservation and restoration work that can never end is just one example; a problem that is only containable by selective judgements. To some extent a similar philosophy has to govern any acquisitions policy, because there have to be priorities over what is purchased, and what temptations are resisted.

For well over fifty years the Department of Printed Books, responsible for most books and bindings (others belong to the Department of Oriental Printed Books and Manuscripts, and the Department of Manuscripts), has aimed at collecting representative examples of the work of bookbinders from all countries and all periods. In practical terms this has meant limiting itself largely to European and American bindings from roughly the third quarter of the fifteenth century to the present.

Modern bindings form part of the collection of historical bindings, and are considered in their historical context, which means that the same criteria for buying are applied. The technical and artistic quality of the binding is obviously important and so is its place in the history of bookbinding as a whole. However, because these funds come from the same budget it can mean that the sudden availability of (for example) an important collection of French bindings of the seventeenth century could deprive the library of any modern bindings at all in that financial year. Certain old bindings may never appear again, whereas modern bindings continue to be produced; but inevitably the Library misses out on opportunities to acquire new work by younger binders before the value of that work starts to appreciate. Another inhibiting factor is that the Library is very conscious that it is spending public money, and is less likely to gamble on the future significance of a particular binding. It does occasionally commission, but not as part of any comprehensive plan; many bindings which should remain in the United Kingdom will find homes in overseas museums and libraries, particularly in the United States, over the remaining years of the century.

However, one important acquisition in 1983 was the complete set of drawings and 'rubbings' for the entire output of bindings of Edgar Mansfield. The source was Duval and Hamilton, who had earlier commissioned Bernard Middleton to produce the two large boxes to contain them.

The Victoria & Albert Museum is in a similar situation, with only one budget for bindings, from which all purchases have to be made; so it too is constantly 'juggling' with limited funds. However, its policy for commissioning new bindings seems more positive than most in the United Kingdom; which means that its collection of modern bindings by the end of the century is likely to be a little more representative.

Hopefully, long before then, a greater awareness of the scope, beauty and excitement of creative binding will have changed the face of the craft so that such works of art become readily available, and we no longer have to make a special journey to one of the major museums or libraries to find examples.

Some interesting bindings for *Alice*. For the two-volume set of *Alice's Adventures in Wonderland* and *Through the Looking-Glass*, illustrated by Barry Moser and published by the Pennyroyal Press, Lage Eric Carlson has designed themes that are harmonious: in the top picture, on the left is the front cover of *Alice in Wonderland*; on the right the back cover of *Through the Looking-Glass*. In the picture below, on the left is the front of *Through the Looking-Glass*; on the right the back of *Wonderland*.

(right) Philip Smith's cover for *Through the Looking-Glass*, illustrated by Ralph Steadman, came from his subconscious – surprising him with its validity. For instance, the chesspiece knight is used as the window in which things happen, because 'knight' in this context means chivalry, which equals 'love' – into which Alice steps. Materials are puckered silver cape sheep, inlays of white calf and black and grey oasis.

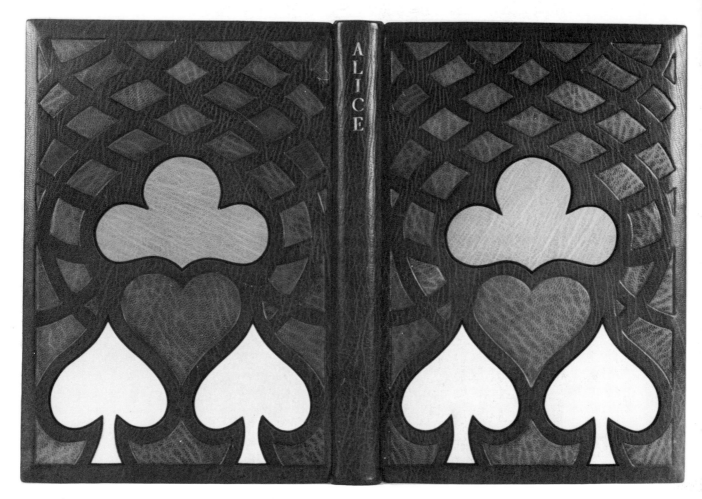

Angela James' simple design for *Alice's Adventures in Wonderland* concentrates on the playing-cards, with onlays of blue and yellow goatskin, and black and cream calf on a covering of red goatskin over sculptured boards. The doublures are of cream calf, with thin black calf edging; the flyleaves are of yellow and blue Japanese paper.

Nowhere is fine binding flourishing better than in Holland and Belgium, where the Flemish Bookbinders' Guild (the Vlaamse Handboekbindersgilde) has several hundred members; it has set up an impressively equipped institute at Ghent, Belgium.

Among Guild members whose work is of special interest is Donatienne van den Bogaert. For her 1983 'double' binding of Gabriel Chevallier's *Les Heritiers Euffe*, she features a 'jacket' of olive-green oasis over covers of olive green and beige stripes *(above right)*. Clouds in varying shades of green are onlaid on the outer cover, but the rooftop design, tooled in gold, interacts with both.

(right)   Pau Groenendijk enjoys arousing the observer's curiosity: this intriguing design for the space adventure story *2001* is made with leather onlaid to a linen binding.

GLOSSARY

Bands   Cords on which a book is sewn/or the bands on the back produced by the cords and showing through the leather.

Dantelles   Border on outer edge of doublure.

Doublures   Inside face of covers, especially when lined with leather and decorated.

Fillets   Impressed straight lines, or the rotating tool for producing them.

Finishing   Ornamentation of book cover, by tooling, lettering etc.

Forwarding   The process of binding and covering prior to finishing; general assembly of book.

Gauffering   Decoration of the gilded edges of book with finishing tools.

Marbling   Colouring of paper (usually doublures and endpapers) in imitation of marble graining.

Maril   Method of mixing (patented by Philip Smith) leather waste and white emulsion, which when dried and pressed into slabs of rock-like coloured leather, produces an inbuilt random pattern.

Morocco   Goatskin leather (originally produced in Morocco), later imitated in sheep or lamb skin, and the most commonly used leather.

Panel stamps   Large metal blocks, cut or engraved with a pictorial or decorative design, usually stamped on cover by press.

Pointillé   Dotted decoration in gold.

Tooling   Decoration with finishing tools, ie rolls or stamps.

Gold tooling   Gold leaf impressed with heated tools.

Blind tooling   Impressing without gold.

SELECTED BIBLIOGRAPHY

Burdett, E., *The Craft of Bookbinding*, David & Charles, 1975, 1982

Clements, J., *Bookbinding*, Arco Publications, London, 1963

Cobden-Sanderson, T. J., *Journals* (2 vols), Macmillan, 1926

Cockerell, D., *Bookbinding & The Care of Books*, London, 1901 (recent editions include 5th, Pitman, 1953; also paperback, 5th revised, 1978)

Cockerell, D., *Some Notes on Bookbinding*, OUP, 1929

Cockerell, S. M., *The Repairing of Books*, London, 1958

Designer Bookbinders, *Modern British Bookbindings* (bound catalogue), London, 1971–2

Franklin, C., *The Private Presses*, Studio Vista, London, 1969

Harrop, D., *History of the Gregynog Press*, Private Libraries Association, 1980

Johnson, A., *The Thames & Hudson Manual of Bookbinding*, London, 1978

Lucie-Smith, E., *World of the Makers*, Paddington Press, London, 1975

Mansfield, E., *Modern Design in Bookbinding*, Peter Owen, London, 1966

Middleton, B. C., *A History of English Craft Bookbinding Technique*, Hafner, London & New York, 1963, 1978

Middleton, B. C., *The Restoration of Leather Bindings*, American Libraries Association, Chicago, 1972, 1984

Nixon, H., *Styles & Designs of Bookbindings from 12th to 20th centuries*, Broxbourne Library, 1961

Robinson, I., *Introducing Bookbinding*, Batsford, London & Watson-Gupthill USA 1968; reprinted Oxford Polytechnic, 1984

de Sausmarez, M., *Basics of Visual Form*, Studio Vista, London & Van Nostrand Reinhold, NY, 1975

Smith, P., *New Directions in Bookbinding*, Studio Vista, London & Van Nostrand Reinhold, NY, 1974

Smith, P., *The Book: Art & Object*, London, 1982

Titcombe, M., *The Bookbindings of T. J. Cobden-Sanderson*, British Library, 1984

INDEX